REGIONAL INTEGRATION AND TRADE LIBERALIZATION IN SUBSAHARAN AFRICA

Volume 4: Synthesis and Review

REGIONAL INTEGRATION AND TRADE LIBERALIZATION IN SUBSAHARAN AFRICA

VOLUME 1: FRAMEWORK, ISSUES AND METHODOLOGICAL PERSPECTIVES
Edited by Ademola Oyejide, Ibrahim Elbadawi and Paul Collier

VOLUME 2: COUNTRY CASE-STUDIES
Edited by Ademola Oyejide, Benno Ndulu and Jan Willem Gunning

VOLUME 3: REGIONAL CASE-STUDIES
Edited by Ademola Oyejide, Ibrahim Elbadawi and Stephen Yeo

VOLUME 4: SYNTHESIS AND REVIEW
Edited by Ademola Oyejide, Benno Ndulu and David Greenaway

Regional Integration and Trade Liberalization in SubSaharan Africa

Volume 4: Synthesis and Review

Edited by

Ademola Oyejide
Professor of Economics and Director of
the Trade Policy Research and Training Programme
University of Ibadan
Nigeria

Benno Ndulu
The World Bank Group
Tanzania

and

David Greenaway
Professor of Economics
CREDIT
University of Nottingham
England

First published in Great Britain 1999 by
MACMILLAN PRESS LTD
Houndmills, Basingstoke, Hampshire RG21 6XS and London
Companies and representatives throughout the world

A catalogue record for this book is available from the British Library.

ISBN 0–333–66107–9

First published in the United States of America 1999 by
ST. MARTIN'S PRESS, INC.,
Scholarly and Reference Division,
175 Fifth Avenue, New York, N.Y. 10010

ISBN 0–312–21772–2 (Vol. 4)

Library of Congress Cataloging-in-Publication Data
Regional integration and trade liberalization in subsaharan Africa.
v.<4>;cm.
Includes bibliographical references and index.
Contents: — Vol. 1. Framework, issues and methodological Perspectives / edited by Ademola Oyejide, Ibrahim Elbadawi and Paul Collier — Vol. 2. Country case-studies / edited by Ademola Oyejide, Benno Ndulu and Jan Willem Gunning — Vol. 3. Regional case-studies / edited by Ademola Oyejide, Ibrahim Elbadawi and Stephen Yeo — Vol. 4. Synthesis and review / edited by Ademola Oyejide, Benno Ndulu and David Greenaway
ISBN 0–312–17321–0 (v. 1).—ISBN 0–312–21769–2 (v. 2).—ISBN 0–312–21771–4 (v. 3).—ISBN 0–312–21772–2 (v. 4)
1. Africa, Sub-Saharan—Economic integration. 2. Africa, Sub -Saharan—Economic policy. 3. Africa, Sub-Saharan—Foreign economic relations. I. Oyejide, T. Ademola. II. Elbadawi, Ibrahim. III. Collier, Paul.
HC800.R448 1997
337.67—dc21 96–49387
CIP

This book is printed on paper suitable for recycling and made from fully managed and sustained forest sources.

10 9 8 7 6 5 4 3 2 1
08 07 06 05 04 03 02 01 00 99

Printed and bound in Great Britain by Antony Rowe Ltd, Chippenham, Wiltshire

Contents

List of Tables

List of Abbreviations

ADB	African Development Bank
AERC	African Economic Research Consortium
AMU	Arab Maghreb Union
APEC	Asia-Pacific Economic Community
ASEAN	Association of South East Asian Nations
CBI	Cross-Border Initiative
CEAC	*Communauté Economique d'Afrique Centrale* (Central African Economic Community)
CEAO	*Communauté Economique de l'Afrique de l'Ouest* (Economic Community of West Africa)
CEMAC	*Communauté Economique et Monetaire d'Afrique Centrale* (Economic and Monetary Union of Central Africa)
CFA	*Communauté Financière en Afrique*
CMA	Common Monetary Area (formerly Rand Monetary Area, now Multilateral Monetary Area)
COMESA	Common Market for Eastern and Southern Africa
EAC	East African Community
ECOSOC	United Nations Economic and Social Council
ECOWAS	Economic Community of West African States
EMS	European Monetary System
EU	European Union
GATT	General Agreement on Tariffs and Trade
GDP	gross domestic product
GNP	gross national product
IBRD	International Bank for Reconstruction and Development
IFI	international financial institution
IGO	inter-government organization
IMF	International Monetary Fund
ISI	import-substitution industrialization
LPA	Lagos Plan of Action
MFA	Multi Fibre Agreement
MMA	Multilateral Monetary Agreement
NAFTA	North American Free Trade Agreement
NGO	non-government organization

OAU	Organization for African Unity
OECD	Organization for Economic Co-operation and Development
PTA	Preferential Trade Area for Eastern and Southern African States
SACU	Southern African Customs Union
SADC	Southern African Development Community
SADC	Southern African Development Co-ordination Conference
SAP	Structural Adjustment Programme
SSA	SubSaharan Africa
TNC	transnational corporation
TPRM	Trade Policy Review Mechanism
UDEAC	*Union Douanière et Economique de l'Afrique Centrale* (Central African Customs and Economic Union)
UDEAO	*Union Douanière de l'Afrique de l'Ouest* (West African Customs Union)
UEMOA	*Union Economique et Monétaire Ouest Africaine* (West African Economic and Monetary Union)
UMOA	*Union Monétaire Ouest Africaine* (West African Monetary Union)
UNCTAD	United Nations Committee on Trade and Development
WTO	World Trade Organization

List of Contributors

Paul Collier	University of Oxford; The World Bank, Washington
David Greenaway	University of Nottingham
Jan Willem Gunning	Free University of Amsterdam; Centre for the Study of African Economies
G.K. Helleiner	University of Toronto
Colin McCarthy	University of Stellenbosch
Benno Ndulu	Former Executive Director, African Economic Research Consortium; The World Bank Group, Tanzania
Séamus O'Cléireacáin	Columbia University
Ademola Oyejide	University of Ibadan

1 Introduction and Overview

Ademola Oyejide, Benno Ndulu and David Greenaway

1.1 INTRODUCTION

This volume contains the five chapters that synthesize the products of the collaborative research project on Regional Integration and Trade Liberalization in SubSaharan Africa sponsored by the African Economic Research Consortium (AERC) and other collaborating institutions. The volume takes several specific issues researched in the project beyond the synthesis stage to the identification and survey of various options that could define the way forward.

This is the fourth and final volume in the series that present various aspects of the collaborative research project. Volume I focuses on conceptual issues and methodological perspectives that underlie the entire project. Volume II presents an analysis of country-specific trade liberalization experiences; while Volume III contains the analysis of regional integration experiences.

This chapter introduces and reviews the five papers presented in this volume. One of these reviews the African regional integration experience with a view to offering proposals for the future evolution of African regionalism; two address the issue of trade liberalization in Africa, one reviews past experiences and draws lessons while the other examines various options regarding future trade liberalization efforts in the continent; and finally, two papers address several aspects of Africa's relations with the rest of the world: one provides a comprehensive survey of options while the other suggests a specific Africa–Europe linkage. Taken together, the five papers offer different perspectives on three key issues. First, they discuss whether, to what extent and how trade liberalization could be used as an instrument for opening up Africa. Second, they offer views regarding the need for linking and the mechanisms with which Africa can be linked together. Third, they examine various options for linking

Africa with the world. The overview of the papers that follows is broadly organized around the three issues.

1.2 OPENING UP AFRICA

The current position regarding trade liberalization in Africa can be viewed from two contrasting perspectives. The chapters by Séamus O'Cléireacáin and Gerry Helleiner speak to these perspectives. O'Cléireacáin (Chapter 3) conveys the half-empty cup view and thus suggests that the speed and durability of trade liberalization in Africa lag behind most other developing countries. As a result, the pace of change in Africa falls well short of the recent experience of East Asian and Eastern European countries. Furthermore, many African countries were less open in the early 1990s than they had been three decades earlier; while the vigorous political debate that has accompanied economic reform in other regions appears lacking in most parts of Africa.

The half-full cup perspective in Helleiner's contribution (Chapter 5) indicates that African countries have already gone some way towards liberalizing their own external trade regimes. In the process, they have achieved substantial success in removing controls and/or replacing them with tariffs and/or currency devaluation. They have also simplified customs duties and their administration, increased relative price of exportables *vis-à-vis* non-tradeables, and reduced anti-export bias within the tradeables sector.

There is more unanimity of views regarding the reasons for the current state of trade liberalization in Africa. Chapter 6, by Ademola Oyejide, and Chapter 5 both stress the difficulties confronting reform of trade regimes in Africa. These difficulties are traced to several factors, including the use of trade policy instruments to serve multiple objectives, the heavy reliance of African countries on trade taxes to generate government revenue and the realistic concerns that rapid import liberalization might cause serious fiscal deficits and balance-of-payments problems. Helleiner and Oyejide both argue that many of Africa's import control measures respond to balance-of-payments pressures rather than import-substitution objectives. Hence it would be incorrect to conceptualize import-control liberalization purely in terms of the cost of protectionism.

O'Cléireacáin (Chapter 3) explains what he considers to be Africa's slow speed of trade liberalization essentially in political economy terms. In this connection, he suggests that sustainable economic reform requires an enabling environment of stable legal and political institutions where regulatory decision-making is transparent and predictable. This presumption translates into a close relationship between speed and durability of economic reform and political liberalization. It follows therefore that since much of Africa is typified by severe restrictions in the political and civil liberties of economic agents, progress toward a more rational trade policy is understandably slow. In more specific terms, O'Cléireacáin argues that Africa is plagued by the emergence of both weak states and weak markets in the context of which market distortions generate rents that are required for retaining political power. Complicated, arbitrary and non-transparent trade policy regimes thus provide avenues for corruption; while proposals for reducing or simplifying trade laws pose an obvious threat to those whose income is derived from policy-induced rent. There is therefore a strong and entrenched resistance against trade liberalization and the process may have to be phased in gradually over many stages.

What should guide the speed and focus of future trade liberalization efforts in Africa? Helleiner believes that there should be no hesitation in unilateral trade liberalization in African countries where controls, administrative complexities and misaligned exchange rates create socially costly interferences in their economic relationships with the rest of the world. But the focus and extent of any such liberalization should be carefully considered. This consideration should bear in mind the two contrasting views on the subject. One approach argues for full and immediate trade liberalization. This view recognizes that there may be sound theoretical grounds for government intervention and that some governments have intervened successfully. But, based on their past experience and current capacity for policy design and implementation, this approach suggests that African governments are unlikely to intervene successfully and should therefore refrain from doing so.

The alternative approach described by Helleiner's in Chapter 5 would consciously seek to make transactions between individual African countries and the rest of the world directly functional to their long-term development objectives. This approach has several attributes. First, it would involve selective and differential incentives and disincentives. Second, it requires being implemented by an activist state. Third, it calls for closer co-operation and coordination between the state and indigenous private firms as both interact with external economic agents in the process of building up indigenous technological capacity and development-supportive institutions.

In a further articulation of this alternative approach, Oyejide (Chapter 6) argues that the primary focus of African trade policy debate on the import regime fails to recognize adequately the important role of exports not necessarily as a technology transfer vehicle but more significantly as the primary source of financing the indispensable bottleneck-breaking and technology-bearing imports. Since a successful and sustainable import-liberalization programme requires successful exports, export promotion should precede import liberalization to ensure that an earlier and robust export supply response can generate the resources for financing further and more sustainable import liberalization. In the same vein, Helleiner associates productivity increases with imported inputs and argues that the focus of African trade policy reforms should be on the acquisition of foreign exchange through exports and foreign direct investment, particularly the latter, which frequently can bring other key inputs along as well. In addition, Helleiner believes that export liberalization is unlikely to cause serious transitional problems and suggests that this should occur and be firmly established before a major import liberalization is attempted.

In any case, according to Oyejide, further trade policy reforms in Africa should be rooted in an outward-orientated development strategy which also reflects each country's initial conditions and industrialization potentials. Trade policy reform, as an integral part of a comprehensive development strategy, should focus on restructuring the existing manufacturing sector to improve its efficiency and on altering the incentive regime to provide exporters with access to inputs at international prices net of tariffs and indirect taxes. The justifiable concern for the survival and growth of an efficient manufacturing sector in African countries as an important component of overall development makes the case for non-zero import tariff levels and a non-uniform import tariff structure. But concerns of allocative efficiency demand that the level of import protection should be moderate (say 25–30 per cent), the tariff structure should be simple, and that there should be only a limited number of tariff rates (perhaps three to five). In addition, Oyejide suggests the use of appropriate proactive measures to assist manufacturers and exporters to cope with the production and learning-by-doing associated with manufacturing and the difficulties of gaining access to the technology and market information needed to establish footholds in international export markets.

Helleiner would also situate future trade policy reform in the context of Africa's longer-run development objectives. According to him, Africa's comparative advantage now and in the near future lies with primary production. Hence, the region's best strategic course is to build on its primary production base, bearing in mind that the greater the growth in the agricultural sector the better are the prospects for more-than-proportionate growth in manufacturing and relative growth in the size of the industrial sector.

But Helleiner also notes the risks attendant on specializing in primary production, a set of activities with few dynamic possibilities that is therefore not conducive to the productivity increases and indigenous learning which a self-sustaining development process requires. While lamenting the absence of a clear-cut indication from the theoretical and empirical literature concerning the appropriate policy stance in this kind of situation, Helleiner concludes against leaving everything to the market and comes out in favor of conscious governmental encouragement to promote activities with more dynamic possibilities. More specifically, he urges support for research and development, training, education and infrastructure, as well as the use of the more direct instruments of subsidies, tax concessions preferential credit and procurement policies. Arguing that the building of appropriate capabilities and institutions may be as critical to success as the incentive structures, Helleiner suggests that totally level playing fields may not always be appropriate, especially in the circumstances of Africa, where local capacity-building is of such dominant importance.

In summary, a few concluding remarks can be drawn from the chapters that address the issue of trade liberalization as a means of opening up the African economies. First, there has been significant trade liberalization in many African countries, although there remains a lot to be done in this direction. Second is the need to recognize the constraints that would create difficulties for further and deeper trade liberalization and the need to take complementary measures that help to relax these constraints before further liberalization can be effected. Third, further trade liberalization should be viewed as an integral part of Africa's long-term development strategy rather than in isolation. The objectives of development should, in this context, determine the role of trade policy as well as the focus and extent of trade liberalization. Fourth, in terms of sequencing, trade policies that liberalize and promote exports should be designed and implemented; these should take root and yield results to provide the resources necessary for financing further import liberalization. Finally, while the ultimate tariff structure could reflect selective and differential incentives and disincentives, it would need to be simpler, more transparent, more stable and more predictable than in the past.

1.3 LINKING AFRICA TOGETHER

The patent desire and associated efforts to link the countries of Africa together have a long history that predates the transformation of many of them from colonies to independent political entities. Regional integration and co-operation arrangements, in one form or the other, have been the principal instruments for the sustained efforts aimed at linking Africa together, either within specific subregions or continent-wide.

Colin McCarthy's chapter (Chapter 2) reviews this history and makes several observations. First, he notes that the keen interest in regional integration in Africa has not been matched by worthwhile result, as most of the integration schemes have not been able to achieve their stated objectives. Second, not only have the high expectations placed upon the regional integration arrangement not been fulfilled, the schemes themselves seem to have become stumbling blocks rather than building blocks in the effort to link Africa together. Third, and perhaps surprisingly, in spite of the obvious failures and lack of progress with regional integration in Africa, the glamour of the idea as a potent linking mechanism appears undiminished. The signing in 1991 of the Abuja Treaty to establish the continent-wide African Economic Community by the year 2025 is a clear indication of the continued hold of the regional integration idea on the minds of African leaders.

McCarthy suggests that the regional integration movement in Africa has been motivated by strong political considerations. The desire for African unity, the need to create new political structures out of the colonial heritage, and the feeling that Africa needs a strong regional body to articulate its views and protect its interests in international political and economic negotiations are important concerns that have influenced the thinking of the proponents of regionalism in Africa. Grafted to these basically political motives for regional integration is a fundamental economic rationale: that the small size of the typical African economy provides the principal explanation for the adoption of economic integration as an instrument for overall economic development.

In this context, regional integration is, inherently, an economic construct even though it may be driven by a strong political motivation. It is against this background that McCarthy poses his fundamental question: whether regional integration is inherently an economically viable mechanism in the African context or whether the problem lies in ill-conceived, badly designed and inadequately implemented regional integration arrangements.

McCarthy finds faults with both the conception and design of most of Africa's regional integration schemes. He also agrees with the general perception that many of them have been badly or inadequately implemented. Conceptually, regional integration was perceived as an inward-looking instrument of industrial development. In this context, the principal goal of integration and growth in intra-regional trade is economic development and structural transformation through industrialization; while the main role of integration is to aggregate the small individual economies into larger regional markets. This approach has been rendered impotent by two problems. First, while the regional economy is much larger than the individual economies, the combined market is still not large enough to promote high levels of industrial development through import substitution. Second, the establishment of these larger integrated regional markets has remained an elusive goal in various parts of Africa.

In terms of design, the apparent preference for formal trade and factor market integration mean-that rather ambitious models of regional integration has usually been adopted. Unfavourable structural factors characterizing Africa, such as the competitive nature of primary production, small size, low per capita income, limited manufacturing capacity, weak financial sectors and poor transportation and communications infrastructure make these ambitious models of regional integration especially problematic. In any case, African integration schemes have suffered from endemic implementation lapses emanating from lack of political will to carry out agreed commitments in the face of ensuring loss of national sovereignty, absence of adequate technical and management expertise, expectations of loss of fiscal revenue on trade taxes, and uncertainty over the distribution of the gains and losses of integration. The problems associated with the conception, design and implementation of most of the existing set of African regional integration schemes implicitly suggest broad ingredients of the way forward. In terms of conception, it is suggested that regional integration should broadly stress outward-orientation while its design should reflect the minimalist approach. This implies a modest function-based co-operation between countries focused on joint implementation of identified projects and schemes, particularly in the area of transportation and communications infrastructure. McCarthy suggests that the minimalist approach would provide greater flexibility and pragmatism and serve as building block for eventual market integration following the elimination of the key infrastructural constraints that currently confront intra-regional trade and factor flows in Africa. Gerry Helleiner's chapter offers a similar view in this respect; it sees the need for the creation of larger regional political and economic units, not necessarily as platforms for preferential trade arrangements but more importantly as a means of realizing the under-utilized potential for broad co-operation in all economic affairs aimed at promoting overall economic development in Africa by building intra-regional trade infrastructure and taking advantage of growth 'spillovers'.

1.4 LINKING AFRICA WITH THE WORLD

There is growing concern that Africa has been and continues to be marginalized in the world goods and capital markets. Africa's share of world trade is the lowest among the developing regions of the world while it is virtually rationed out of the global foreign direct investment flows. Africa's marginalization may be related to its weak linkage with the global economy at a time when global economic integration (that is, the widening, deepening and intensification of world-wide linkages in trade, investment and finance) is increasing rapidly. To the extent that there may exist a close and positive relationship between global integration and growth, it becomes an important policy issue to examine how, to what extent, and through which mechanisms African countries should link themselves to the rest of the world.

While not denying the possibility that closer integration with the global economy could yield some growth-enhancing benefits, Gerry Helleiner warns that increasing globalization poses considerable dangers for the typical African country. In his view, the global economy remains crisis-prone and unstable; it has the potential of imparting greater vulnerability to individual nation-states through external shocks. Rather than embarking on a head-long rush into a closer embrace with globalization, what is considered to be more appropriate is a selective approach that assigns an important role to risk aversion and risk management. It is argued, in particular, that given their weak strength in the global economic system, it is unlikely that African countries would derive more significant gains from integration into the global economy on a full and equal basis than they currently enjoy. While a more transparent, predictable and rule-based global trade and economic system would help the weaker African participants, total harmonization of their domestic policies with international standards could be problematic.

It is recognized, however, that a significant proportion of private transactions between Africa and the rest of the world is mediated through transnational firms. In addition, expanded foreign direct investment represents an indispensable avenue for future African economic growth. The credibility (that is, stability and predictability) of African trade (and other policies) is a crucial factor in attracting and retaining such investment. In other words, unless private decision-makers perceive the new incentive structures as likely to be sustained, they are unlikely to respond in the expected development-enhancing way.

This is precisely the problem on which the contribution of Paul Collier and Jan Gunning focuses. In Chapter 4 they pinpoint the fear of policy reversal as one of the key factors deterring the revival of investment in Africa, in spite of recent and, in several cases, substantial policy reforms. In this context, and according to Helleiner, if the current African problems of inadequate and ineffective response to policy reforms are attributable to the lack of credibility and instability of its governments and policy regimes, close external linkages that promote African policy credibility and stability could play a useful role.

An 'agency of restraint' is what Collier and Gunning call the institution that helps to strengthen policy credibility and prevent disastrous reversals. They argue that African governments cannot be effectively restrained by domestic agencies until there is more firmly established and enforceable confidence in the rule of law in African countries. They therefore suggest that African governments will have to rely on external agencies of restraint in the meantime. To be effective, these institutions should satisfy two conditions. First, they must have and be prepared to use sanctions that are sufficient to deter unacceptable behaviour. Second, the interests of the agency must be congruent with those of the governments that voluntarily choose to be restrained by it. This implies reciprocity. Governments that are bound by the rules of this agency participate in writing and enforcing those rules.

It seems obvious that African regional integration schemes have not set for themselves agency-of-restraint functions and, given their endemic implementation problems, it is unlikely that they can play this role in the near future. In the absence of an African agency of restraint, two proposals have been made. One is based on more active participation of African countries in an existing global institution. The other envisages the establishment of a new reciprocal relationship between Africa and Europe.

In Chapter 3, O'Cléireacáin suggests that African countries gave up a good opportunity of using active participation in the Uruguay Round of multilateral trade negotiations under GATT/WTO as a mechanism for reinforcing the credibility of their reform effort. To the extent that internationally registered tariff bindings lock in reform on the domestic front and can be used to ward off local lobbies seeking further protection, the WTO framework provides a mechanism for importing credibility for a trade reform programme. The clear message is that African governments could derive considerable benefits from an active participation in WTO which is geared specifically to the strengthening of policy credibility.

The Collier–Gunning proposal is more radical. It envisages small groups of African countries setting up customs unions among themselves under supranational control and then negotiating reciprocal free trade with the European Union. Several advantages are claimed for this proposal. First, it would amount to an effective agency of restraint within which African policy reversal would elicit a heavy penalty, that is the loss of unrestricted access to the European market. Second, the arrangement would achieve as much as Africa could hope to gain under global liberalization, given Africa's current and potential export market access requirements. Third, it would ensure that Africa is not locked out in a world of powerful trade blocs ineffectively policed by the WTO. Fourth as the region's policy regimes become more credible it may attract foreign direct investment to Africa from firms wanting to set up and produce for Africa as well as those wishing to produce for Europe from an African base.

Both of these proposals are not without their problems. It is not self-evident, for instance, that African countries have the capacity to participate fully and effectively in the WTO without substantial technical assistance and, perhaps, some co-operation at the regional level. With respect to both the WTO and a reciprocal Africa-Europe linkage, Helleiner warns against adherence to 'harmonized' standards that may be inappropriate for specific country circumstances.

To a considerable extent, Africa is already linked to the rest of the world. Recent policy reforms across the continent suggest a radical shift away from its historic inward-looking development strategy in favour of greater outward-orientation. This shift implies increasing integration into the global economy in matters of trade, investment and finance. But because globalization can cause serious problems of economic management, the globalization process needs to be carefully managed given the vulnerability of fragile African countries to external shocks that may be generated by that process.

2 Regional Integration in SubSaharan Africa: Past, Present and Future

Colin McCarthy

2.1 INTRODUCTION

In subSaharan Africa (SSA) the keen interest in regional economic integration has not been matched by results. The story that can be told is largely one of failure – that much is clear from reading the contributions to this AERC volume.

But looking back on recent developments it is possible to identify some positive events. Perhaps the most important has been the democratization of South Africa and consequently the possibility of greater involvement of the continent's largest and most developed economy in the economic affairs of Southern Africa, and even further afield. The restructuring in 1992 of the Southern African Development Co-ordination Conference (SADCC) into the Southern African Development Community (SADC) and South Africa's entry into SADC in November 1994 as the organization's eleventh member mirrored the new dispensation in the region. The current renegotiation of the Southern African Customs Union (SACU) agreement to adapt Africa's oldest functioning customs union to meet the requirements of the post-apartheid situation is also of considerable importance, especially in view of the enhanced role that can be envisaged for SACU (Fine and Yeo, 1997; Mwase and Maasdorp, 1998). In West Africa the revision in 1992 of the Treaty of the Economic Community of West African States (ECOWAS) as an attempt to revamp the Community could turn out to be an important development (Jebuni, Ogunkola and Soludo, 1999). In francophone Africa, the devaluation of the CFA franc in January 1994 and the formation, also in 1994, of the West African Economic and Monetary Union (best known by its French acronym of EUMOA) and the planned Economic and Monetary Union of Central

Africa (French acronym CEMAC), as part of a re-alignment of the regional integration arrangements of the francophone states, also represent significant events.

The future of the CFA zone remains uncertain, especially and somewhat paradoxically, because of the anchor role of France and the French franc in the zone. This role has to be reconciled with France's strong commitment to the European Union and monetary union in Europe. But the recent developments in the CFA zone have at least been dynamic; together with those in Southern Africa, as well as the efforts to revive the East African Community, they can be listed as positive elements in a checklist of African regional integration. These developments, with the exception of ECOWAS, do not form part of the original framework of the Lagos Plan of Action (LPA) adopted in April 1980. By and large the unifying framework of regional unions in the LPA as 'a centerpiece in the grand strategy for Africa in the pursuit of development' (Johnson, 1991, p. 2) never materialized.

The sad but sobering part of the lack of progress with regional integration in SSA is that the high expectations that existed for integration as a means to improve the economic performance and welfare of the poorest part of the world have remained unfulfilled. Independence from colonial rule came late to Africa and, as will be argued later, ambitious integration arrangements were an important element in schemes to build a continent confident in its political independence and economic development. Unfortunately, it can be argued, the integration schemes adopted were more in the nature of stumbling blocks than economic building blocks.

It is also important to bear in mind that some integration arrangements, notably those in francophone Africa and East Africa as well as SACU, were colonial legacies that were merely carried over, with adjustments, into the post-colonial era. Regional integration, therefore, was not a 'new' concept for independent Africa. However, the mechanism found a fertile breeding ground in independent Africa where the proliferation of integration arrangements, especially during the 1970s, produced the largest number of such arrangements found in any region of the world. Unfortunately, many of these are ineffective or dormant. Nevertheless, in spite of the lack of progress with regional integration in SSA, its glamour has not diminished (Lyakurwa, McKay, Ng'eno and Kennes, 1997). This 'glamour' kept the ideals of the LPA alive and culminated 1991 in the signing by the African heads of state of the Abuja Treaty to establish a Pan-African Economic Community by the year 2025. Pan-Africanism, as an expression of continental identity and coherence distinguishes regional integration in Africa from other regions in the developing world. This political inspiration, strongly supported by the rational idea that integrated markets could circumvent the small size of the typical African economy as a constraint on economic development, explains the continuous popularity of integration schemes in SSA. The idea appeals regardless of the poor track record of integration, the widespread inability to meet the targets set for integration schemes and the very likely prospect that a continent-wide economic community will not materialize.

In considering the failure of regional integration in SSA the fundamental question is whether integration is inherently an economically viable mechanism in the African context, or whether it is merely a case of integration arrangements that have been ill-conceived or not properly implemented (Lyakurwa, *et al.*, 1997). Looking into the future from the perspective of past experience, it will be argued in this chapter that the latter is a more likely explanation. If properly conceived – that is, with sound national economic development policies and more modest schemes within the framework of regional co-operation as a first step towards integration – regionalism can contribute to a more prosperous SSA.

2.2 AFRICAN EXPERIENCE WITH REGIONAL INTEGRATION

In tracing the development of regional integration in Africa a number of features can be identified that have given the African experience, although similar to that of other developing areas (notably Latin America), a particular character. These features are discussed in this section as a backdrop for the consideration in the remainder of the chapter of possible future developments and the problems that will have to be solved.[1]

Rationale of Integration

Regional economic integration represents an exercise in international economic relations, driven by economic mechanisms, but frequently with political objectives as the underlying driving force. There is even the view that the new regionalism can be distinguished by its emphasis on the non-economic and political dimensions: 'Political ambition of creating territorial identity, political convergence, collective security and regional coherence now seem to be the primary, neo-mercantilist goals of the new regionalism' (Mistry, 1995, p. 13). However, it is difficult to see why this should be regarded as a distinguishing characteristic of the *new* regionalism. Political issues played a considerable, if not initiating, role in many schemes of the 'old' regionalism. The European Union, the leading case of post-war regional integration, originally got started through concern for security in the face of the cold war threat and as an effort to maintain peace between countries (France and Germany) that history has shown to be war-prone. In Asia, the Association of South East Asian Nations (ASEAN) was created in 1967 mainly to enhance political stability in the region.

In Africa, also, political considerations have motivated economic integration. African unity, the formation of regional political structures in a process of post-colonial consolidation, and the creation of regional blocs for effective use in international political forums and in negotiations with economic powers in the developed world underlie much of the thinking of the proponents of integration in Africa. Okolo (1990, p. 25) is very explicit in this regard when he describes the political goal of ECOWAS as 'the need to have an institutionalized instrument to maximize the bargaining position of the smaller and weaker West African states *vis-à-vis* the bigger and more powerful industrialized nations of the world and, particularly, to extricate the region's economy from western neocolonial control'. Elsewhere, explicit security factors have laid the foundations for regional co-operation. SADC(C) is an example of an organization that was established on the basis of security considerations, namely, the desire to become less dependent on apartheid South Africa in a period of strong economic and military confrontation in the region (Lyakurwa, 1997). There are also clear indications that SADC will become an important instrument for resolving regional political conflicts. In north Africa, the establishment of the Arab Maghreb Union (AMU) in 1989 was to a large extent driven by the politico-economic consideration of creating a body that could bargain collectively with the European Community with which 70 per cent of the AMU countries' trade takes place. Furthermore, the founding of the AMU followed the major *rapprochement* in

1988 between Algeria and Morocco, who both saw the new arrangement as a framework within which the long dispute over the western Sahara could be resolved. These considerations prompted Mortimer to refer to the AMU as 'more a diplomatic than an economic construct' (1993, p. 18).

But politics apart, regional economic integration remains an economic affair and any integration arrangement must be justified in economic terms. In a sense regional integration can be seen as a political construct held together by economic cement. If the 'cement' fails the construct fails; hence, the importance attached to economic integration and co-operation as the defining feature of integration exercises. The African experience is no exception. In fact, the emphasis on the economic rationale of integration, as is common in all developing regions where integration is seen as a means to facilitate economic development and growth, has been an important element of African integration exercises.

African economies, while sizeable in terms of population, are small in terms of GDP; average income levels are low. South Africa's gross domestic product (GDP) of US$104 bn (1992) – which is approximately three and a half times larger than the Nigerian GDP, the second-largest economy in SSA – is slightly smaller than the Norwegian GDP of US$113 bn. The GDP of SSA, excluding South Africa, is approximately US$134 bn, which is only 30 per cent larger than the South African GDP and smaller than the Belgian GDP (World Bank, 1995).

The small size of African economies has been the main explanation for the adoption of economic integration as an instrument of development. The emphasis falls on the dynamic outcome of regional integration and its impact on industrialization, which has been regarded as the engine of economic development. In this view the principal goal of integration and growth in intra-regional trade is economic development and structural change through industrial growth; in the words of Mytelka (1975, p. 240): 'Integration in many developing areas of the world is . . . a paradigm for industrialization'. In Africa the importance of industrialization found expression in the designation of the 1980s as the "Industrial Development Decade in Africa" in the LPA. According to Ravenhill (1986, p. 91) 'Industrialization is very much the plan's panacea'.

The link between regional integration and industrialization must be sought on the demand side of the growth equation. Investment in physical and human capital is an important force on the supply side, but viable and growing markets, in turn, are prime determinants of investment. Investment does not occur in a vacuum, but is initiated by a desire to create capacity to produce for an identified market. Add a dose of export pessimism by believing that developing countries will find it difficult, if not impossible, to access the markets of the industrialized world with manufactured exports, and it follows that import substitution is the only viable 'demand source' of manufacturing growth, at least during the initial stages of industrialization. At this point efficiency and economies of scale enter the scene with the argument that the small size of most developing economies, notably those in Africa, restrict the ability of these countries to benefit from lower unit costs in a process of inward-looking development. Extending the market through regional integration suggests itself as the logical way to enable manufacturers to produce at lower unit costs for a larger protected market. The latter is regarded as a more viable source of the benefits of economies of scale than the world market because of the anticipated problems of access and the higher transaction costs of producing for the world market.[2]

Trade expansion takes place through import substitution within the regional market. Since trade diversion is the driving force of development-orientated market integration, welfare gains are not crucial. Nevertheless, previously unemployed resources are put to use in high-cost industrial production without a loss of output elsewhere; real income grows, even though the resources are used inefficiently in world market terms. On the basis of this kind of reasoning it has been concluded that 'under conditions of underdevelopment inefficient production provides more gains than no production at all' (Axline, 1984, pp. 8–9). Regional integration in this way becomes an inward-looking instrument of industrial development, diverting trade from cheaper sources in the rest of the world to higher-cost producers within the union.

In Africa, however, the economies are so small that even when combined the larger entity remains small by world standards and, furthermore, constrained by the high costs of transport and communication due to poor facilities in these sectors. At US$ 80 bn the GDP (1989) of the 16-member ECOWAS, with a population of 180 million, is smaller than that of Denmark with its GDP of US$90 000 bn, population of 5.1 million, and an integrated infrastructure producing comparatively low-cost transport and communication services. While the sum of the markets is much larger than the individual markets of the participating economies, thus raising the potential for inward-looking industrial growth not possible in the individual states, the combined market is still not large enough to reach high levels of industrial development through import substitution.[3] Of course, even this is hypothetical, since the creation of these single markets has remained an elusive goal in Africa.

Nevertheless, the small size of African economies and the observation that in the long run the prices of many primary commodities tend to decline in relation to those of manufactures have converted African leaders, the Organization of African Unity and the UN Economic Commission for Africa (ECA) to economic integration as the road to development. The ECA emulated the Economic Commission for Latin America and became the champion of regional integration, already in the mid-1960s propagating the division of Africa into regions for the purposes of economic development (Okolo, 1990; Ravenhill, 1986). This strategy was eventually embodied in the LPA.

But development-orientated market integration, aimed at the creation of a larger market for import-substituting industrialization, does not facilitate the establishment of producers that are competitive in international markets. Regional trade liberalization is not a substitute for an outward-looking development strategy, and if it is accepted that a better economic future for Africa will require that trade opportunities be exploited world-wide rather than within any particular geographical area (Rimmer, 1988), the inward-looking regional option has held little hope for SSA. Also, the protectionist measures created a bias against agricultural production and exports (DeRosa, 1997). Furthermore, the national development strategies did not create a leading role for private sector initiative. Parastatals were established to provide the driving force of industrialization, and state-led development, in the words of Jebuni, Ogunkola and Soludo, 'literally killed the private sector' in West Africa, leaving only some remains 'dependent on the state and the rents from the import-licensing system'.

Integration Models

Since industrialization behind a common external tariff has been of primary concern in SSA, a feature of regional integration efforts has been the ambitious models adopted. In most instances a preference has existed for formal trade and factor market integration, which in terms of the classical linear model means that the formation of a common market has been the popular final objective (Johnson, 1991). The dominance of the common market as coveted integration objective was encapsulated in the LPA. African governments pledged themselves explicitly in the plan to an African Common Market as the first step to an African Economic Community. With the exception of SADCC, the regional arrangements in SSA have not accepted the more modest goal of economic co-operation. But even SADCC, when it was transformed in 1992 into SADC, adopted a trade protocol that has trade integration as its objective. Since then, an agreement on the free movement of people has also come under consideration. The Preferential Trade Area for Eastern and Southern Africa (PTA) has made little progress towards regional free trade, but in 1992 nevertheless raised its sights to become a common market. In December 1994 the PTA was transformed into the Common Market for Eastern and Southern Africa (COMESA) when the treaty to this effect was ratified by the required number of member states.

The common market goal has remained elusive and overambitious, with very few arrangements having achieved their integration targets within the timetables adopted. In the case of ECOWAS, for example, negligible progress was been made, from its inception in 1975, to have a free flow of trade and common external tariff (that is, a customs union) by the original target date of 1990. Only the Southern African Customs Union (SACU) and the Central African Customs and Economic Union (UDEAC) have common external tariffs. In the case of SACU the common external tariff – that is, the South African tariff which doubles as the SACU tariff – is a legacy of the colonial period. In the case of UDEAC, described by Fine and Yeo (1997) as 'a virtually moribund trade association', the common external tariff has been negated by the ability of the member states to set different tax rates on products traded within the union (World Bank, 1991). As far as COMESA is concerned, most countries are far behind schedule in the programmed reduction of tariff and non-tariff barriers and it is doubtful that COMESA will achieve its goal of a common market by 2000 (Kasekende and Ng'eno, 1999).

Monetary integration becomes part of the linear process of trade integration when participating countries move toward the common market model (which has a free flow of capital between countries), and finally an economic union when fiscal and monetary harmonization takes place. In Africa, monetary and trade integration has been non-linear, moving on two tracks in two prominent cases, namely the CFA (*Communauté Financière en Afrique*) zone and the Common Monetary Area (CMA) in southern Africa. In both these cases of successful monetary integration a strong link exists with a dominant partner, which in the case of the CFA zone is external (O'Connell, 1997).

Members of the Economic Community of West Africa (CEAO), also belonged to the West African Monetary Union (UMOA), with a dualism of economic policy that existed in the form of a co-ordinated monetary policy falling within the ambit of community institutions on the one hand and on the other an economic and fiscal policy that was the responsibility of the individual member states. A clear need emerged for a co-ordinated overall economic policy (M'bet, 1999), which explains the establishment in 1994 of UEMOA. UEMOA now has the task of harmonizing the management of public finance, debt, external payments and pricing policy in the member states (M'bet, 1999). The intention is that convergent monetary and fiscal policies will enhance the long-term viability of the integration arrangement.

The members of the CFA zone, with the exception of ex-Spanish Equatorial Guinea, share a common colonial history and bond with France as their former colonial power and owe the monetary union to this link. A unique feature is that the 13 members of the CFA zone do not as a group belong to an overarching trade integration arrangement but are linked into different arrangements. The seven countries of the CFA zone that form UEMOA do not share their membership in ECOWAS with the other six members of the CFA zone.

In Southern Africa the four-member Common Monetary Area (CMA) is closely paralleled by the five-member SACU, with the CMA consisting of all SACU members excluding Botswana. The Botswana pula is convertible, which means that SACU operates with convertible currencies and therefore at a level of integration that does not exist elsewhere in SSA. The South African rand is the anchor currency of the CMA in a way that effectively integrates the capital and money markets of Lesotho, Namibia, and Swaziland into the South African financial system (Mwase and Maasdorp, 1999). An interesting feature of the CMA is that it operates in terms of the Multilateral Monetary Agreement (MMA) of 1992, supported by bilateral agreements between South Africa and its partners. The bilaterals have been designed to meet the requirements of each of the partners within the broader ambit of the MMA. This particular arrangement might prove to be a useful and flexible formula to facilitate the widening of integration in Southern Africa, especially in the more stable macroeconomic environment brought about by the recent fall in the inflation rate in South Africa to below 10 per cent.

Constraints on Progress

Progress in regional integration must of course be reflected in increases in the share of intra-regional trade in total foreign trade. As a continent, Africa's trade has never been characterized by a high degree of recorded intra-regional trade. Moreover intra-regional trade as a share of total foreign trade has always been low (8.4 per cent in 1993) when compared with Western Europe (69.9 per cent), Asia (49.7 per cent), North America (33 per cent) and Latin America (19.4 per cent) (World Trade Organization, 1995, p. 39). This low level of intra-regional trade reflects the dominance of Africa's trade with the EU and the USA in what has come to be known as a 'hub-and-spoke' trade pattern (Baldwin, 1997), that is, the focus of African trade on the north (the 'hub') – primary commodities traded for the importation of manufactured goods – accompanied by little trade among the African economies (the 'spokes').

Structural factors such as the competitive nature of primary-producing, small, low-income economies with little manufacturing capacity, weak financial sectors, and a poor intra-state and inter-state transport and communications infrastructure all contribute to economies that have little to trade with each other but are locked into a North–South trading relationship. The features of lack of development, poverty and the size drawback underlie the findings of gravity model research indicating that 'the low share of intra-SSA trade is more than fully accounted for by the fact that SSA-countries' natural trading partners, those that are close, are also countries that are very poor and quite small and hence have very little trade potential' (Foroutan and Pritchett, 1993, p. 89). This, of course, does not deny that it could also be concluded on the basis of normative arguments 'that SSA is not sufficiently integrated and that intra-SSA trade is "too little"' (Elbadawi, 1997).

It follows as a matter of composition that the continental situation will also be reflected in Africa's regional arrangements.[4] These arrangements have the lowest levels of recorded intra-regional trade of all integration exercises, with shares of intra-regional exports typically below 5 per cent (Foroutan, 1993; Elbadawi, 1997; Kasekende and Ng'eno, 1999). This signifies that regional integration has failed in SSA. Okolo (1990), referring to the West African experience, observed the following in this respect: 'although the desire to reduce external dependence provided the impetus toward integration, there has been no significant change in the low level of trade that characterized West African intra-regional interaction in the past'.

The exceptions to the general case of low intra-regional trade have been the CEAO and SACU, both having shares of intra-regional trade above 10 per cent of total trade. In the case of CEAO, intra-regional exports in 1990 were 11.3 per cent of total exports (De La Torre and Kelly, 1992, p. 30). SACU is the shining star of African intra-regional trade: intra-regional exports were 18.4 per cent and 20.3 per cent of total exports in 1990 and 1994.[5] The CEAO was noted for its currency convertibility and capital mobility – unlike the UDEAC, which also shared this feature but found itself on the opposite side of the spectrum of success – that was supported by significant labour mobility, a pragmatic product-by-product approach to intra-regional trade liberalization, and a compensation system that addressed the issue of the distribution of integration gains (M'bet, 1999). SACU's success with intra-regional trade is explained by the development of an integrated economy in the region characterized by a dependency relationship between South Africa and the smaller SACU members. This relationship is reflected in a massive trade balance in favour of South Africa (Hirsch, Holden, Jenkins and Bleaney, 1999). It has the further characteristic of a regional hub-and-spoke pattern; there is very little trade between the smaller SACU members, with the dominant flow of trade centred on South Africa as hub and the four smaller members as spokes.

The reasons for the poor progress with integration referred to earlier, namely the limited trade potential and the structural features of the typical African economy, can be extended by turning the focus to the political economy of integration decisions and management. The conclusion of integration agreements is only the first step; these agreements have to be implemented and in Africa the degree of implementation of trade liberalization within the regions has generally been low. Two prominent African arrangements, ECOWAS and UDEAC, have been noted for their 'almost complete non-implementation of intra-area liberalization' (De La Torre and Kelly, 1992, p. 32). From its inception until 1990 ECOWAS

was preoccupied with the establishment of institutions and the ratification of protocols (Jebuni, Ogunkola and Soludo, 1999). In COMESA, the commendable clearing house, established in 1984 to facilitate the settlement of claims arising from transactions among member countries, has not had the positive impact on intra-regional trade hoped for. After a promising start the value of clearing house transactions started falling after 1989 (Kasekende and Ng'eno, 1999).

But why have integration agreements not been implemented? It is not easy to provide a succinct answer to this question, since the problem has many facets, many of them interrelated. A fair approximation would be to emphasize the lack of political commitment to carry through integration programmes in the face of the ensuing loss of sovereignty, the absence of the required technical and administrative expertise (Ostergaard, 1993), and the uncertainty over the distribution of the gains and losses of integration. It must be emphasized that the lack of political will as it is used here is not the old 'red-herring' variety, which Ravenhill identifies as a poor explanation for the failure of regional integration arrangements, namely, a lack of faith because it is not realized that multinational cooperation and integration are absolute imperatives (1986). What is of concern is the post-agreement lack of enthusiasm when the political realities of implementing an integration arrangement strike home.

It should be noted at the start that acceptance at the national level of import-substituting industrial development policies created a bias against regionalism. Kasekende and Ng'eno (1999) point to the fact that these policies produced unfavourable external balances, fixed exchange rates, foreign exchange controls and over-valued regional currencies. Hence, it was cheaper to import intermediate goods than to develop them locally. The shortage of foreign exchange led to a preference for what would offer the best credit resources. These were mostly in the industrialized world, thus supporting the development of the hub-and-spoke pattern of trade. Import-substitution strategies at a national level also proved to be an impediment to the evolution of a regional perspective on development. In the post-independence years inward-looking development was characterized by strong feelings of economic nationalism and rent-seeking activities generated by protectionism. A strong neighbourhood effect developed, with every country's belief in these policies being reinforced by similar beliefs held by other countries in the region. Jebuni *et al.* (1999) argue that in the case of ECOWAS no country could detach itself from its nationalistic agenda to champion the cause of the community. This attachment to the national agenda at the cost of the region might also explain the reported resentment against Zimbabwe within COMESA, where Zimbabwe has been accused of being more interested in exporting to member countries than importing from them (Neube *et al.*, 1999).

This bias against regional integration was strengthened by the inevitable demand for the sacrifices of some control over economic policies that directly affect the populations of the participating countries. Establishing a common external tariff and regional free trade, co-ordinating macroeconomic policies (monetary, fiscal and exchange rate), harmonizing industrial development policies (which might even ambitiously include a regional plan for the location of industry), and promoting intra-regional labour and capital mobility are all required to give effect to the intended programmes. But these entail a sacrifice of national sovereignty and presumably the creation of a supranational regional authority with real powers. Many political leaders find it difficult to accept this, especially in the African setting where political and government institutions still lack maturity and skill, where political life is strongly influenced by personalities, and where ethnic diversity and the fragile economic environment encourage a short-term horizon in policy formulation.[6] Also, it can be hypothesized that a sacrifice of sovereignty requires, somewhat paradoxically, a strong state and confident national governance, which includes an effective bureaucracy.[7] Even then, as the experience of the EU has shown, ceding sovereignty is not easy. But it is more difficult to envisage the successful integration of weak states; the creation of integration arrangements cannot serve as a substitute for poor or weak national governance. How, for example, can COMESA succeed if seven of its members – Zaire, Rwanda, Burundi, Sudan, Somalia, Ethiopia, and Eritrea – can be described as being in domestic disarray and not in a position to manage their national polities and economies properly, let alone contribute meaningfully to COMESA and accept the commitments implied by membership of a regional integration arrangement (Mistry, 1996)? Finally, in respect of political will, it is also difficult to integrate and cede sovereignty if the member states are divided on major political and ideological issues.

Many SSA integration arrangements do not meet these requirements. In West Africa, for example, integration is hampered by the existence of weak states. As might be expected, SSA integration arrangements are not characterized by strong supranational bodies. Integration institutions are virtually all intergovernmental. This allows governments the opportunity to avoid a loss of sovereignty through unilateral decisions on the application of regional agreements.

Political will is also affected by expectations of gains and losses from integration, and regional interests tend to be given priority only if they promote national interests. Countries will participate actively in regional integration exercises if they believe that they will benefit. Moreover, a belief exists that integration should lead to balanced growth within the region. However, if left to the operation of the market, cumulative forces driven by economies of scale will in a single market cause development and growth to gravitate towards the more-developed participating countries, thus causing inequality in the distribution of the costs and benefits of integration. Polarized development, differences in perceptions of benefits and of the time scale within which the benefits are expected to materialize, as well as political expediency in the face of pressure group activity, explain why the unequal distribution of costs and benefits is probably the most important reason for the major conflicts experienced by developing countries participating in integration schemes.

Africa has been no exception in this regard. For ECOWAS the polarization impact of the dominant economy, Nigeria, is an important explanation for the lack of progress, while similar conditions have contributed to the demise of one of Africa's most promising integration arrangements, the East African Community. On the other end of the spectrum, as noted earlier, CEAO seems to have done better than most regional schemes because the two more prosperous members, Côte d'Ivoire and Senegal, have been willing to shoulder a larger compensating burden. SACU, in turn, can credit its longevity as a customs union of unequal partners to compensatory payments that South Africa makes to the smaller members of the union.

Finally, a large number of African countries depend for their fiscal revenue on taxes on international trade. Although regional trade liberalization would affect this revenue negatively, thus causing countries to prefer trade with the rest of the world to regional trade, Jebuni *et al.* (1999) point to the fact that this outcome is not inevitable. Nevertheless, expectations of such revenue losses, and other perceived problems such as a negative impact on the external balance, could contribute to a lack of commitment to an integration arrangement.

Institutional Proliferation and Overlapping Membership

Variable geometry, multiple speed and concentric circles are fashionable terms, generated by the European experience, that describe flexibility in the tiers of integration within a broad arrangement. This flexibility originated in the need to accommodate and reconcile the widening of the European Union and the phenomenon of member-selectivity in the deepening of the Union, a development that will become even more meaningful when monetary integration takes place.

In principle, variable geometry cannot be faulted, but it should not be confused with the phenomenon of overlapping membership, which has become a feature of integration in SSA.[8] However, there are examples of tiers of integration within single integration arrangements which could develop into arrangements that resemble variable geometry. The experience in Southern Africa is a case where overlapping membership occurs among arrangements at different levels of integration. All the members of SACU are also members of SADC, while four SACU members are also members of the CMA. Within SACU, effective (*de facto*) labour market integration exists between Lesotho and South Africa, which means that these two countries for all practical purposes form a common market. This construct of overlapping membership is functional and could form the basis for the development of viable economic co-operation structures in the region, perhaps even along the lines of a Southern African Economic Region proposed by Fine and Yeo (1997). Along similar lines, it has been suggested that integration could deepen within SACU to a common market or even an economic union between some of its members (that is, variable geometry within SACU), with SACU forming an association agreement with the remaining SADC countries or the southern countries of the PTA along the lines of the EC/EFTA agreement for the European Economic Area (Maasdorp, 1994, p. 26; Mwase and Maasdorp; 1999). Variable tiers of integration can also provide for the expansion of existing arrangements. In a consultative document prepared for the annual meeting of the SADC in January 1995 it was proposed that, together with free labour and capital mobility, SACU be expanded by drawing in the other SADC countries to create a common market in the region. Widening SACU within the framework of the current SACU Agreement (which is being renegotiated) is easier said than done. But the principle remains valid: variable geometry can be used to accommodate expanding membership at different levels of integration.

Overlapping membership, however, could cause complications and inconsistencies when countries belong to different integration arrangements with similar agendas and objectives but still on the same tier of integration. If overlapping membership occurs in arrangements with more or less the same objectives and anticipated development path, conflicting interests will develop and progress with integration will suffer. It is difficult to envisage how the SADC and COMESA, given both their convergence to sectoral co-operation and trade integration, can live and prosper with their overlapping membership. Whereas the predecessors of SADC and COMESA had complemented each other – the first geared to functional co-operation to become less dependent on apartheid South Africa, and the second to trade integration among a much broader group – the adoption in 1993 and 1994 by both organizations of trade integration *en route* to an economic union of all members in 25–30 years time, has placed the two on a competitive footing. Restructuring seems inevitable if institutional rivalry between COMESA and the SADC and malaise in integration are to be contained. The fact that South Africa has joined the SADC but not COMESA is bound to favour the SADC and the view has been expressed that South Africa's decision is 'another pointer to the eminent collapse of COMESA' (Kasekende and Ng'eno, 1999).

In West Africa the establishment of UEMOA, with programmes parallel to those of ECOWAS, is difficult to reconcile with the revised ECOWAS treaty, which provides that the latter 'shall ultimately be the sole economic community in the region for the purpose of economic integration' (Onitiri, 1997).

It should be noted that for both the incompatible SADC/COMESA and UEMOA/ECOWAS relationships, the apparently more viable agreements – the SADC and UEMOA – have created questions about the long-term viability of two arrangements that form part of the Lagos Plan/Abuja Treaty vision for regional integration in SSA. In both cases challenges are presented to a top-down approach to regional integration and co-operation by arrangements that share strong common links and a measure of political cohesion. In both cases also a strong power is present; in the case of UEMOA, France as an external power and in the case of the SADC, South Africa, initially as the force that instigated the common political bond for the SADC and now the dominant economy of the community.

2.3 CORE–PERIPHERAL TENSIONS IN REGIONAL INTEGRATION

Turning now to the future against the background of the experience with regional integration in SSA, a perusal of the papers in this project and other sources suggests a number of important issues. One of these is the problem of polarized development, a problem that will be relevant if regional integration and development are centred on a strong economy as the regional core. A theoretical diversion into location theory in an overview of the core–peripheral relationships associated with market integration serves as an introduction to this analysis. The new situation created by post-apartheid South Africa is brought into the picture since it introduces important dimensions to regional development. The underlying theme of the discussion is that regional co-operation arrangements will not be viable in the long run if regional growth is not equitably distributed among participating countries.

Theoretical Aspects of Polarization

According to conventional neoclassical theory, polarized development in an integrated market should not be a problem, and to the extent that it does occur it would be a passing phenomenon. In this model world of mobile capital and labour, full employment and free competition, market forces will channel resources to lagging regions and so ensure the removal of regional disparities.[9] However, these conditions are rarely, if ever, met and disparities have become a characteristic of regional growth patterns, within national states and among integrating national states.

Two strands of theoretical thinking, one in the field of trade theory and the other in the theory of regional economics and development, provide the basis for the contention that there are forces at work that cause regional growth paths to diverge and that the notion of the economy as a self-adjusting mechanism is false.

Neoclassical trade theory, with its predictions of gains for all trading countries when they enter into free trade under conditions of different factor endowments and constant returns to scale, has increasingly come to be questioned by economists, who emphasize the existence of increasing returns to scale, imperfect competition and external economies.[10] If constant returns to scale apply, average production cost does not vary with changes in the volume of output. Under this assumption – a fundamental premise of neoclassical trade theory – the price mechanism reigns supreme as the equilibrating force that will clear markets. With increasing returns to scale, average cost falls when output expands, allowing firms to grow at the cost of competitors by producing more in a market that can only support a limited number of producers. In such a market, production does not respond continuously to price movements or to shifts in demand. External economies refer to the benefits gained by individuals and firms from the activities of other parties. A well-known example is the diffusion of knowledge because of technological advances made by others.

This line of analysis anticipates additional welfare gains for countries and groups from trade, including lower unit cost of production, enhanced competition, increased product diversity and greater intra-industry specialization. But it also supports the contention that international trade will not benefit all participants equally. The larger and more industrially advanced a country is, the more likely it is to expand its production on the basis of increasing returns to scale and external economies, especially those based on technological competition.

External economies also arise through regional agglomeration. These economies introduce the second strand of thinking that supports the contention of a self-enforcing tendency towards regional disparities through trade growth, namely, Myrdal's concept of cumulative causation through backwash effects in regional growth (1957). This could be described as a 'snow-ball' growth hypothesis: size begets size, with a region that, in the words of Kaldor (1970, p. 340), 'is initially more developed industrially' gaining 'from the progressive opening of trade at the expense of the less developed region whose development will be inhibited by it'.

The driving force of cumulative growth is increasing returns to scale in production (internal economies of scale) and agglomeration advantages, that is, lower production costs because of the proximity of other firms and industries (external or agglomeration economies), a factor that has long been noted by geographers (Krugman, 1994). The increased specialization that accompanies the fragmentation of production and other processes into more specialized activities leads to greater division of labour and more inter-firm transactions. This, and the new developments in production management of 'just-in-time' systems of stock control, encourage agglomeration of large industrial networks. The larger regions also have labour market advantages with the accumulation of skilled workers, among others, through in-migration. The centre also has an environment that stimulates the development of innovation leadership and expertise that, according to an OECD report, 'grows by the cumulative effects of learning, scale and sector cross-fertilisation' in a geographically concentrated area 'contrary to the assumptions of the orthodox theory of comparative advantage' (quoted in National Economic and Social Council, 1989, p. 318).

Polarization in Southern Africa

Where, from the perspective of regional integration in SSA, does this theoretical overview of the geographic dispersion of economic activity lead us? The first point to make is that it partly explains the 'hub-and-spoke' nature of SSA trade patterns discussed earlier, which is a special form of polarization or core–peripheral relationship. Most African economies lack the critical economic mass that can generate external economies, especially the economies of scale required for competitive production. These are located in the European hub at the cost of development in the African spokes.

An important exception is South Africa, which has developed a relatively diversified economy with its own core–peripheral relationships in Southern Africa where it is the regional hub with regional spokes, as noted earlier with respect to SACU. The region has an integrated transport and communications infrastructure centred on South Africa, a situation of dominance that served as an important consideration in the establishment of SADCC in 1980. The combination of this infrastructure, proximity and knowledge of markets and the ability to produce marketable goods have provided South African producers with a competitive advantage in the regional market and the benefits of polarized growth in South Africa's metropolitan areas. The outcome has been the development of a mercantilist trade pattern in the region with a trade balance heavily in favour of South Africa; exports from South Africa to the region exceeded imports from the region by a factor of nearly four in 1994. Hirsch *et al.* (1999) report that South African trade penetration of the Southern African region increased over 250 per cent in the period 1988–94 thus posing a threat to its competitors in the region, notably Zimbabwe, which is the only other country in the region with a reasonably well developed and diversified manufacturing sector.

It can be hypothesized that polarized development in an integrated Southern Africa has two dimensions: one is the concentration of production in South Africa *vis-à-vis* the neighbouring states, and the other is the metropolitan concentration in South Africa itself *vis-à-vis* the country's rural areas. South Africa may be the focus point of development in Southern Africa, but it should be borne in mind that large rural areas of the country are economically underdeveloped, with people living in conditions of poverty comparable to or even worse than those found elsewhere in Africa.

At this point factor flows can be brought into the story. The flow of labour to high-wage, developed countries and areas from low-wage areas or countries, characterized by gross unemployment and underemployment, as well as capital moving in the opposite direction on the basis of return differentials, is supposed to counter the regional skewedness of growth. Labour mobility, earlier experience in West Africa has shown (see Okolo, 1990), is politically difficult and sensitive, and with the large inflow of migrants into South Africa, there are signs that it will also be a sensitive issue in Southern Africa, with the tightening of procedures to close borders to illegal immigrants as a possible outcome (Hirsch *et al.*).

But capital flows could be a different matter. The argument here would be that the South African business sector, which is already active in the region, can make a significant contribution to the development of production capacity in South Africa's neighbouring states. Recent news reports have frequently portrayed South African business people as increasingly active in the region and further afield in SSA. An example of this investment in production capacity is the announcement by two South African financial institutions – Rand Merchant Bank and the Credit Guarantee Insurance Corporation – of their pending investment in the construction of a major hydroelectric facility at Sounda Gorge at the confluence of the Niari and Kouilou rivers in the Congo.

But even northbound South African capital flows might not be without their sensitivities. There is anecdotal evidence that South African firms are investing in the region to escape the perceived inflexibilities of the labour market and the relatively high labour costs in their own country. In one case a company closed its clothing factory in the rural, poverty-stricken Eastern Cape and relocated to Malawi. This reminds one of the prediction of the Krugman–Venables model of regional location that the difference between the developed centre and the underdeveloped periphery leads to a wage gap: 'when transport costs fall low enough, industry abruptly pops up in the low-wage country' (Krugman, 1994, p. 22). The investment in Malawi is a striking example, of capital and therefore job opportunities moving from one poor and underdeveloped area to another, with Malawi benefiting at the cost, not of developed metropolitan South Africa, but of underdeveloped rural South Africa. The explanation for this development must in part be sought in the centralized determination of wage levels for industrial sectors, which means that wages cannot play an equilibrating role in regional development within South Africa. The sensitivities mentioned above may arise when the trek of South African capital and firms into other areas of Africa becomes so significant that it raises the opposition of workers and South Africa's well-organized trade union movement.

Dealing with Polarization

Polarized development will remain an important issue with a debilitating impact on the progress made with integration in SSA. In theory, the problem can easily be dealt with. A policy framework for the evaluation of measures to counter polarization can be derived from the functions of public policy: that is the allocation, stabilization and redistribution functions.

A number of inferences can be drawn from applying the three functions to the economic integration of national states. Integration leads to greater interdependence. However, interdependence in trade and factor flows not only leads to greater room for specialization and efficiency gains to be had from allocating sources to the most productive use, but also enhances the intra-regional transmission of economic instability, which creates the need for co-ordinated stabilization policies. The function of redistribution becomes relevant when it is accepted that no a priori reason exists why the gains from integration will translate into gains for all participating countries, thus justifying policies that will redress polarization. When independent countries enter into integration arrangements, or any co-operative arrangement that aims to open trade, all three functions of public policy become valid.

The allocation function is the relevant one when the redressing of polarization is left to regional factor flows. If the more-developed countries have higher wage levels and lower returns to capital, investment flows to the less-developed countries can lead to greater regional equality. Policies and programmes can be devised to encourage cross-border investment through the removal of obstacles to regional investment and trade. The Cross Border Initiative (CBI) for Eastern and Southern Africa, sponsored by the European Union, the World Bank, International Monetary Fund and the African Development Bank, represents an exercise of this nature. The programme aims to hasten progress towards liberalization achieved by national structural adjustment programmes and the regional integration arrangements (Mwase and Maasdorp, 1999; Kasekende and Ng'eno, 1999).

Instead of leaving it to market-based factor flows, a policy of compensatory regional transfers, associated with the redistribution function, can be used to address polarization, As noted earlier, SACU is a prominent example of compensatory transfers that become part of the recurrent revenue of the recipient countries. These payments are determined by a formula that contains an enhancement factor to compensate the smaller SACU members for the effects of polarization, the price-raising impact of trade diversion, and the loss of fiscal independence (McCarthy, 1992).

While the logic of compensation is easy to understand, the practical problems that arise when the political dimension is introduced can prove very difficult. How does one quantify the extent of the compensation required? In the case of SACU the persistent complaint of the smaller members has been that the compensation for the drawbacks of being in a customs union with much larger South Africa has not been sufficient. In South Africa, in turn, a strong suspicion existed in some influential circles that SACU membership was costing South Africa too much (Mwase and Maasdorp, 1999). Fiscal pressures and a direct and visible drain on the treasury have to measure up against the indirect and difficult-to-quantify benefits of the captive market created for South African industry. Although economists could agree that net benefits could justify substantial compensation under these circumstances, the finance minister and cabinet coleagues will find it difficult to accept the transfers when they seek to balance the books in the face of a constituency which itself is poor and in need of redistribution through public expenditure. It is difficult to envisage that this issue will be less problematical in democratic South Africa. In fact, it would be reasonable to expect the opposite.

But a second option is to deal with polarization through the use of corrective policies that address the underlying problem of regional imbalance. Measures are adopted to enable the less-developed members of integration arrangements to gain their fair share of the industrial growth brought about by integration. These policies, it has been argued, 'represent a higher level of integration since they respond to more fundamental causes of unequal development in the region' (Axline, 1984, p. 94). However, the 'higher level of integration' and the political commitment this would require in addressing 'fundamental causes' of unequal development do not necessarily mean that corrective measures will be strongly dirigiste. In fact, a range of corrective measures that vary in their degree of *dirigisme* can be distinguished. At the one extreme, less-developed member countries could merely be excluded from the free trade condition of membership, either by being placed in a different category of membership that is given a longer period to move to free trade within the integration arrangement, or by creating a special arrangement that would allow them countries to protect selected industries or sectors. The transfer tax provided for in the Treaty of East African Co-operation was an example of a policy instrument, essentially a tariff, designed to provide the industries of the less-developed members of the East African Community with protection against the industries of the more-developed member states (Kasekende and Ng'eno, 1999).

A second possibility is to establish a regional development bank, mostly financed by the more-developed member states, that would give less-developed members privileged access to funding for development projects. Moving up the scale of *dirigisme*, regional institutions and the headquarters of regional services may be located in the less-developed member countries. The most extreme form of *dirigisme* is a regional industrial policy that seeks to allocate industries to member countries. To be really effective this naturally requires a high degree of industrial planning, with inequality in regional development prevented through the distribution of industrial development that stems from integration among the member countries.

While these methods can be used to compensate for polarized development or provide for greater equality in growth, the process of dealing with polarization will remain difficult. A number of qualifications can be made in this regard.

First, differences could exist between the regional and national dimensions of the public policy functions, specifically the redistribution and allocation functions. Bearing in mind that economic asymmetry is the instigating force that underlies polarization and the need to address the distribution of net benefits, it is possible to envisage a situation where differences between economies are so large that the importance of equity at the regional level could be outweighed by efficiency considerations at the national level. Although the context is somewhat different, the possible clash between policy options was highlighted by Robson (1988) in an analysis of the CEAO. Robson considered the wide disparity between the industrial development achieved in the Côte d'Ivoire and that of the other member states who have 'probably no practicable alternative' to inward-looking policies. He concluded: 'If policy reappraisals were to induce Ivory Coast to adopt a more outward-looking policy, in the interest of restoring its economic growth which has been severely curtailed in the last few years, the required changes in the structure and level of its tariffs and incentives might well not be compatible with the needs of CEAO' (Robson, 1988, p. 216). In this example the growth and development needs of the Côte d'Ivoire are perceived to demand policy measures that are not optimal for the CEAO. It is not difficult to imagine that the redistributionist policy measures required to ameliorate polarization could clash with the different challenges of efficiency facing the dominant member state.

The second qualification ties in with a point raised earlier, namely, that inequality and the position of the poor in the dominant economy could outweigh support for regional equity. The problem of inequality takes on special meaning when the integration area is considered in terms of national and regional differences. As noted earlier with regard to the Southern African situation, agglomeration will take place at the growth poles of the larger, more-industrialized member states and at cost not only to the smaller member states but also to the backward regions of the dominant economy where large numbers of the poor are concentrated. Under these circumstances the more-developed countries, to cite Axline (1984, p. 95), 'may find it politically difficult to transfer gains to other member countries'. If regions and not national states are taken as the constituent elements of an integrated market, a different perspective on the distribution of economic activity can develop. In the European Union, for example, northern Italy contains some of the most prosperous regions in the Union, as defined in terms of a synthetic index of economic activity (Trimble, 1990), while the Mezzogiorno shares with Greece, Ireland, Spain and Portugal the feature of having the highest intensity of regional problems in the Union. In the case of the integration of developing countries the problem is further complicated if, as noted above, the dominant economy, having proceeded further on the road of industrialization, is confronted by efficiency challenges and the need for policy measures that do not correspond with those of the region.

Moreover, it is important to consider that regional economic integration is only one of many causal factors in the growth and development equation. The experience of the fast-growing NICs has shown that factors such as investment growth, a favourable human capital endowment, a dynamic private sector, strategic government intervention in support of profitable private investment and outward-looking development are closely associated with rapid growth. The new growth theories emphasize the importance of endogenous factors in the growth process with the focus on endogenous productivity growth in the wake of investment in research and development and the easier absorption of new technologies in open economies.

Where does this leave regional integration as a growth-facilitating force and how is the impact of regional integration on regional asymmetries differentiated from those of the other growth-inducing factors? Most likely not in a commanding and unambiguous position, and at best not a means that can compensate for inappropriate national policies.

Finally, the idea of the trade-off that is usually said to exist between efficiency (growth) and equity (redistribution) in national policies can presumably also be applied to the integrated market of sovereign states. However, it needs to be emphasized that there is no necessary conflict between efficiency and equity. Experience with national policies has shown that investment in human capital, as the outcome of equity criteria in policy-making, benefits efficiency in the long run; a substitution of equity criteria for efficiency criteria could be a positive-sum game with improvements in both efficiency and equity. This complementary relationship between equity and efficiency criteria has become the hallmark of the policy prescriptions of the Economic Commission for Latin America and the Caribbean (1992). However, this substitution could also lead to a negative-sum game with equity criteria given prominence in a manner that will damage efficiency and, in the long run, also equity (Geiger, 1978). The combination of efficiency and equity criteria in a way that will ensure a positive-sum game can also be applied to regional integration. It is not difficult to envisage a situation in which a due regard for equity in the distribution of the gains from integration will in the long run also enhance the growth of the integrated market as a whole. However, the problem mentioned earlier remains: how does one convince the national constituencies of the more developed economies that long-term benefits will follow the initial costs?

Economic policy is made in the political process, and given the qualifications discussed above, it is clear that in the real world of political economy it could be very difficult to adopt a policy that would address polarization effectively.

2.4 APPROPRIATE INTEGRATION MODELS

The underlying theme of our discussion of the SSA experience has been that regional integration is driven by pan-Africanist ideology of continental unity and a desire to escape the constraints posed by the smallness of economies. But is market integration the most appropriate model on which to base development and growth in a regional setting?

Although the experience in SSA has been poor, the current integration arrangements in Africa have to be accepted as a *fait accompli*. Diversifying industrial growth on the basis of growing intra-regional trade – the final goal of the development-orientated market integration model – has not materialized and calls by Africans for a different approach have become commonplace. The gist of the integration-sceptics' convictions is succinctly reflected in Makhtar Diouf's view that:

> it is time to forget theoretical schemes of the pan-African type (a 'United States of Africa') or the neo-colonial type (a customs union), replacing them with simpler, cheaper, more productive, and more cost-effective models of integration through projects – choosing priority sectors for development (agriculture, industry, power, transportation, and training) and identifying specific, concrete projects in each sector to be implemented on a community basis, with possible financial support from outside. (Diouf, 1990, p. 26)

Not surprisingly, the proponents of a minimalist approach have embraced the SADC(C) with its simple and lean administrative structure as the example to follow.

In considering alternative approaches it will be useful to consider the ultimate rationale for regional integration, which is to make a contribution to sustained economic growth. This raises two issues or questions, the first being the identification of the causes of economic growth and the second the causal relationship between regional integration and these growth factors. This, essentially, is what Fine and Yeo (1997) set out to do in their innovative paper on a suitable approach to regional integration in SSA, which is to be discussed below. Falling back on studies of the East Asian experience, they identify two growth factors: effective macroeconomic management within a framework of credible policy and the rapid accumulation of physical and human capital. On the issue of policy credibility the flexibility of policy reactions to changing circumstances can be added as an additional dimension. Gustav Ranis (1995, p. 54) in a recent review of the Taiwanese and Korean growth experience, came to the following conclusion in this respect:

> What clearly marks off East Asia from the average developing-economy case is the remarkable ability of the authorities to recognize mistakes and quickly take appropriate corrective action. In brief, public policies in East Asia consistently accommodated the changing needs of the economy, rather than specifically directing its path.

It could be argued that modest function-based co-operation, broadly defined as co-operation between independent countries or agencies in identified projects or schemes, would, in eschewing grandiose integration schemes, be a more credible policy suited to circumstances in SSA (McCarthy, 1995). This approach to regional affairs, which these days features prominently in the literature, could take the form of sectoral development through project integration. The scope for trade within the region is broadened by adding what Balassa and Stoutjesdijk referred to as regional goods and services. They described these as goods and services that 'may be provided on a national basis as well as jointly for a group of contiguous countries [but] cannot as a rule be imported from world markets' (Balassa and Stoutjesdijk, 1975, pp. 46–7).[11] These projects could include co-operation in the provision of transportation and communications infrastructure, electricity generation and distribution, the development and management of water resources, and co-operation in the provision of educational and research facilities. Many of these products and services require high-cost and indivisible investment that which will provide lower unit cost when provided on a regional and not a national scale. Thematic co-operation – for example, a regional programme on food security, disease control or a code on cross-border investment and the regional movement of people – would also fit into a scheme of function-based regional co-operation.

Among the advantages of this 'made to order' approach are its flexibility and pragmatism in circumventing the problems posed by nationalism and equity in the distribution of costs and benefits. It is also better suited to deal with the many fiscal, physical and technical barriers to trade that cannot be addressed by trade policy.

Since the focus is on specific tasks, issues are depoliticized and thus present less of a challenge to existing power structures. In time a 'culture' of regional co-operation is created, thus laying the foundation for market integration and the acceptance of the loss of sovereignty this entails. Greater integration becomes a minimalist approach, in contrast to the maximalist approach thus far preferred in SSA. Incremental steps are taken that do not make unrealistic demands on the institutional, technical and political capacities of African states. The targeted nature of the approach also serves as a practical means of including and thereby neutralizing the demands of domestic interest groups and is suited to the creation of the infrastructure and production capacity necessary for growth in intra-regional trade and a successful entry into world markets.

This approach, in broad terms, is not out of touch with the integration strategy the African Development Bank (1993), in a major report, recommended as the most suitable for regional integration in Southern Africa. Sector co-ordination and co-operation are given considerable weight, with an emphasis on incrementalism and open-endedness in terms of membership and flexibility through variable geometry and multi-speed paradigms. In practical terms, as noted above, functional co-operation can also derive significant support from the fact that the SADC presents an example in action. The SADC(C) has not exactly been a success in achieving its main objectives (to become less dependent on South Africa), but the arrangement has succeeded in creating a solid identity with the heads of state of the Southern African countries more personally involved in SADC than in COMESA.[12] South Africa's membership, and its allocated responsibility for the strategic finance and investment portfolio, can help the SADC to build on the foundation laid during the past 14 years. However, this assumes South Africa's enthusiastic participation in the SADC and not the realization of the widely-held perception outside South Africa of a weak commitment by the dominating economy

A second approach would be to maintain a preference for integration, but in line with the new regionalism and its contention that the larger regional market can serve as an entry point into the world market. Regional integration in this guise becomes the instrument of outward-orientated growth and can be seen as a re-action to the fact that import substitution has fallen out of favour with policy-makers. A regional integration arrangement that seeks to facilitate competitive entry into world markets makes more sense in the new policy climate than arguing its merits for import-substituting industrialization. Domestic industries are given the opportunity to cut their competitive teeth in the larger regional market before being exposed to the harsh world of the global marketplace. In contrast to the inward-looking approach, which sees regional integration primarily as a means to effect import-substituting industrialization, primarily, the new regionalism views the larger regional market as the conduit to international competitiveness on the basis of lower unit costs of production.

But why could industry not seek these lower costs in the world market directly? The usual answer to this question is to be found in the lower transactions costs involved in producing for the regional market compared to the world market. Information on prices and consumer preferences are more readily available in the regional context, while transport costs are lower, which all lead to lower transactions costs. As far as most of SSA is concerned, however, this is true in theory but not in practice. Though lower transaction costs can explain the comparative advantage South African producers have in the regional market, the hub-and-spoke pattern of trade between SSA and the industrialized world can in part be ascribed to the high transaction costs of trade among SSA countries. Poor transport and communication links, tariff and non-tariff barriers to trade, weak financial services, and the pervasive lack of sophisticated business skills make for high transaction costs. These supplement the structural characteristics of the neighbouring economies in explaining low intra-regional trade.

Regional integration could contribute to growth and development through the lowering of transaction costs. To the extent that these costs are lower than those encountered in world trade, the regional market can provide a viable gateway to international trade and eventually competitive entry into the world market. But this intention – observed (for example) in Latin America, where MERCOSUR, consisting of Argentina, Brazil, Paraguay and Uruguay, has entry to the world market as its primary goal – is largely absent or played down in Africa. Nevertheless, the economic restructuring programmes adopted in many African countries have international competitiveness as their long-term objective, which means that the national development strategies are out of kilter with the philosophy of inward-looking integration arrangements within which these countries may find themselves.

At this point, however, we may again return to function-based regional co-operation. Much, if not most, of the transaction costs encountered in regional trade can be lowered without entering into formal and ambitious integration arrangements that have the establishment of customs unions or common markets in mind, and can adequately be addressed through regional projects of the kind discussed earlier. Functional co-operation not only broadens the range of tradeable products by adding regional to international goods and services (see n. 11) but also lowers transaction costs, thus providing a politically digestible way to increase intra-regional trade. The development of an integrated transport and communications network can make a fundamental contribution to the lowering of transaction costs by easing the barriers to the movement of goods, services and people (Lyakurwa).

A third approach to regional integration could be the one suggested by Fine and Yeo (1997) as a new approach for SSA. Their proposal is to link regional arrangements in SSA with an external partner (the most plausible being the European Union because of historical and cultural ties and existing economic and institutional links) in reciprocal agreements that will provide a framework for locking the SSA economies into sound and stable macroeconomic policies that can resist strong domestic pressures. This, in turn, will induce faster accumulation of physical and human capital.

Fine and Yeo (1997) present three regional arrangements as apposite examples. The first is francophone Africa, where the establishment of UEMOA has effectively installed France as the external power responsible for surveillance of macroeconomic policies through its underwriting of the common monetary system. The second example would be the establishment of a Southern African Economic Region with South Africa as the regional hub locked into two reciprocal international agreements, one with the GATT (WTO) and the other with the European Union. Together with a number of bilateral agreements, notably between SACU on the one hand and Zimbabwe and perhaps Kenya on the other, and a system of strategic responses to counter polarized growth, these arrangements could provide the framework for ensuring sensible macroeconomic policies. Essentially the proposal for a Southern African Economic Region rests on the dominant position of South Africa as the regional hub, the high degree of integration that already exists between South Africa and the other SACU countries, the use of measures that will facilitate balanced development in the region, and the possibility of using bilateral arrangements within the region and externally with the European Union. The third example is a resurrected East African Community (EAC II), with the possibility of a resurrection seen to be strengthened by developments towards a Southern African Economic Region. Again, the intention would be to use reciprocal agreements with the European Union to establish the latter as the guarantor of sound macroeconomic policies in EAC II.

Bringing the European Union in as an external power through agreements that will ensure sound macroeconomic policies in SSA countries does remind one of the politically indigestible suggestions in some circles that the economic problems of Africa could be solved through the 'recolonization' of the continent. The point cannot be missed that the rationale for selecting Europe as the external anchor is essentially derived from its position as the collective colonial power of the pre-independence era. Simultaneously, it is also possible to see in this anchor role, and in the emphasis placed on South Africa's role in Southern Africa, elements of hegemonic leadership, albeit of the benevolent, and not exploitive, variety. Economic dominance creates a hegemonic position but the relationships among the countries will have a more multilateral character with mutual benefits.

To anchor domestic policy in SSA countries in the surveillance by the European Union as an external power makes eminent sense, but will it work? It is difficult to be optimistic in this respect. In the first place the benefits for Europe of such an approach are not clear. SSA has become quite marginal to the European Union, is not a major market, has lost its political leverage in the post-cold war era and does not represent a real threat as a massive source of migrants. Add the high level of structural unemployment in Europe, the European Union's own inequalities and the resulting policies of economic cohesion, as well as the interest groups that seek to protect sensitive industries, and the prospects for an amicable Europe seem dim. The lethargic progress made in the current negotiations on a free trade agreement between the European Union and South Africa does not instil optimism about a Europe willing to become the external partner in integration arrangements with groupings in SSA.

Finally, an obvious point needs to be made: the two growth conditions that Fine and Yeo (1997) emphasize, namely effective and credible macroeconomic management and the accumulation of human and physical capital, must be based firmly in the national agendas of countries participating in regional arrangements. External anchors will not be maintained unless there is a national commitment to policy objectives. But then, the need for an external anchor would not arise if such a national commitment existed.

2.5 CONCLUSION

Can regionalism facilitate economic growth and development in SSA? Having considered the past experience with regional integration arrangements and alternative approaches, as revealed in these papers and other studies, it is clear that regional integration, with some exceptions, has failed in SSA. Intra-regional trade remains low and economic diversification and development have not materialized. However, this does not mean that the regional option cannot make an adequate contribution. What it does mean is that poor commitment to grandiose integration schemes did not deliver the goods and is unlikely to do so in the future.

Looking back on past developments and hopes, one cannot fail to notice that the integration arrangements associated with the vision of the Lagos Plan of Action are particularly conspicuous in their failure. These arrangements were top-down designs and fundamentally different from, for example, the SADC, which has a greater sense of identity and cohesion.

A number of pointers to a better future can be identified, however. The first is that incrementalism in the development of regional arrangements would be more suitable in building regional cohesion. Incrementalism does not immediately require large and developed institutional capacities, avoids the delusions of grandeur and subsequent disappointments that characterize so many integration exercises in SSA, and can effectively address the limitations on regional trade and factor flows and the development of infrastructure. Second, it would be unwise not to build on certain nuclei of regional economic power, cohesion and external links that exist in SSA. Southern Africa, with South Africa as a benevolent hegemony, francophone Africa where UEMOA represents an important development, and East Africa where the revival of the East African Community could create potential for a brighter future, are all notable examples. Thirdly there is no escaping the reality that good and credible policy starts at the national level. Regional arrangements cannot in the long run impose good policy in a top-down fashion on national governments. But this does not deny that regional and external links can provide discipline in support of domestic policy.

Notes

1. Part of the discussion in this section draws on McCarthy (1995).
2. In the world market, developing country producers have to face established and highly competitive producers; this raises risk and uncertainty. Within the region, information on costs, prices and consumers preferences is more readily available, and transport costs lower.
3. Foroutan, pointing to the fact that in 1989 the combined GNP of all SSA countries (excluding South Africa) was approximately equal to that of Belgium, argues that the small size of combined markets in Africa makes regional integration intuitively appealing. He then says: 'Imagine subdividing Belgium into forty-something independent countries, each with its own isolated goods and factor markets, a different public administration, currency, language, fiscal and monetary authorities, army, plus a very inefficient intercountry transportation network. Economists would contend that the welfare of individuals would surely be reduced' (1993: 234). One cannot disagree with this line of thinking, but it misses the point that subdividing an integrated economic and political entity is fundamentally different from combining such entities.
4. References to the low levels of intra-regional trade refer to recorded trade. Unrecorded trans-border trade, however, by all accounts is substantial and appears to be increasing in most of Africa (Barad, 1990). Naturally, unrecorded trade is especially important between neighbouring states that do not belong to the same customs union or monetary area, for example, between CFA zone countries and non-member states (Azam, 1990). To the extent that unrecorded trade represents smuggling, it is difficult to conceive that it could add significantly to intra-regional trade of an integration arrangement, the proviso being that the

arrangement is characterized by a significant degree of free trade.
5. These estimates are based on a breakdown of SACU trade flows by the Nedcor Economic Unit.
6. With reference to the now defunct East African Community, Hazelwood (1988, p. 174) observed the following on the question of sacrificing sovereignty: 'The importance of sovereignty in the first flush of independence would have prevented any delegation of powers, and gives credence to the view that arrangements which require a surrender of sovereignty if they are to work efficiently – even if they go no further than a commitment to consultation before decisions are taken – are exceptionally difficult for a new nation.'
7. One of the problems new nations face is the absence of an affective bureaucracy. As Landes (1990, p. 10) noted, 'it takes time to create an effective, functional bureaucracy: also to establish a commitment to a larger national identity and purpose'.
8. For example: In Southern Africa Lesotho and Swaziland are members of SACU, the CMA, the SADC, and COMESA; Mauritius is a member of the Indian Ocean Commission, but also of COMESA and since 1995 of the SADC; in West Africa, Benin, Burkina-Faso, Côte d'Ivoire, Mali, Niger, Senegal and Togo are members of the UEMOA and of the ECOWAS; Mauritania is a member of both ECOWAS and AMU.
9. In the neoclassical model the assumption of factor mobility is not necessary to ensure the equalization of factor incomes. As long as there are no barriers to trade the Hechscher–Ohlin theorem, which assumes the free flow of goods across national borders, will bring about the equalization of factor incomes. Workers in one country will therefore not be worse off than workers in any other country.
10. Paul Krugman has been a pioneer in the new developments in trade theory centring on increasing returns to scale and external economies (1981, 1983 and 1987). A succinct and non-technical discussion of the new theory, written from the perspective of regional integration, appears in the Irish National Economic and Social Council's study of Ireland's position in the European Union (1989: ch. 2).
11. Those goods, such as perishables, construction, housing and retail trade, which are normally not traded among countries are described as national goods. International goods are traded in national, regional and world markets.
12. It has been suggested that this can be ascribed to the fact that SADC was established with a political motive under conditions of solidarity, whereas PTA/COMESA was designed by the bureaucracy at the UN Economic Commission for Africa as a geographic component of the grand plan for the African Economic Community and with little regard for shared interests (Anglin in Kasekende and Ng'eno, 1999).

References

Adam, C and F. Musonda (1999) 'Zambia' in Oyejide, A., B. Ndulu and J. W. Gunning (eds.) *Regional Integration and Trade Liberalization in SubSaharan Africa. Vol. 2: Country Case-Studies* (London: Macmillan).

African Development Bank (1993) *Economic Integration in Southern Africa* (Abidjan: African Development Bank).

Axline W. A. (1984) 'Underdevelopment, Dependence, and Integration: The Politics of Regionalism in the Third World', in P. K. Ghosh (ed.), *Economic Integration and Third World Development* (Westport: Greenwood Press).

Azam, J. P. (1990) 'Informal Integration through Parallel Markets for Goods and Foreign Exchange', *The Long-Term Perspective Study of Sub-Saharan Africa*, vol. 4, Proceedings of a Workshop on Regional Integration and Co-operation (Washington, DC: The World Bank).

Balassa, B. and A. Stoutjesdijk (1975) 'Economic Integration among Developing Countries', *Journal of Common Market Studies*, **14**(6).

Baldwin, R. E. (1997) 'Review of Theoretical Developments on Regional Integration' in A. Oyejide, I. Elbadawi and P. Collier (eds.) *Regional Integration Trade Liberalization in SubSaharan Africa. Vol. 1: Framework, Issues and Methodological Perspectives* (London: Macmillan).

Barad, R. (1990) 'Unrecorded Transborder Trade in Sub-Saharan Africa and its Implications for Regional Economic Integration', in *The Long-Term Perspective Study of Sub-Saharan Africa*, vol. 4, Proceedings of a Workshop on Regional Integration and Co-operation (Washington, DC: The World Bank).

DeRosa, D. A. (1997) 'Regional Integration and the Bias Against Agriculture and other "Disadvantaged" Sectors in SubSaharan Africa' in A. Oyejide, I. Elbadawi and P. Collier (eds.) *Regional Integration and Trade Liberalization in SubSaharan Africa. Vol. 1: Framework, Issues and Methodological Perspectives* (London: Macmillan).

Diouf, M. (1990) 'Evaluation of West African Experiments in Economic Integration', in *The Long-Term Perspective Study of Sub-Saharan Africa*, vol. 4 Proceedings of a Workshop on Regional Integration and Co-operation (Washington, DC: The World Bank).

Economic Commission for Latin America and the Caribbean (1992) *Social equity and Changing Production Patterns: An Integrated Approach* (Santiago, Chile: ECLAC).

Elbadawi, I. (1997) 'The Impact of Regional Trade and Monetary Schemes on Intra-subSaharan Africa Trade' in A. Oyejide, I. Elbadawi and P. Collier (eds.) *Regional Integration and Trade Liberalization in SubSaharan Africa. Vol. 1: Framework, Issues and Methodological Perspectives* (London: Macmillan).

Fine, J. and S. Yeo (1997) 'Regional Integration in a SubSaharan Africa: Dead end or a Fresh Start?' in A. Oyejide, I. Elbadawi and P. Collier (eds.) *Regional Integration and Trade Liberalization in SubSaharan Africa. Vol. 1: Framework, Issues and Methodological Perspectives* (London: Macmillan).

Foroutan, F. (1993) 'Regional Integration in Sub-Saharan Africa: Past

Experience and Future Prospects', in J. De Melo and A. Panagariya (eds), *New Dimensions in Regional Integration* (Cambridge University Press).

Foroutan, F. and L. Pritchett (1993) 'Intra Sub-Saharan African trade: is it too little?', *Journal of African Economies*, **2**(1).

Geiger, T. (1978) *Welfare and Efficiency – Their interactions in Western Europe and Implications for International Economic Relations* (London: Macmillan).

Hazelwood, A. (1988) 'The East African Community', in A. M. El-Agraa (ed.), *International Economic Integration* (Basingstoke: Macmillan).

Hirsch, A., M. Holden, C. Jenkins, and M. Bleaney (1999) 'South Africa' in Oyejide, A., B. Ndulu and J. W. Gunning (eds.) *Regional Integration and Trade Liberalization in SubSaharan Africa. Vol. 2: Country Case-Studies* (London: Macmillan).

Jebuni, C., E. O. Ogunkola and C. C. Soludo (1999) 'A Case-Study of the Economic Community of West Africa (ECOWAS)' in A. Ojeyide, I. Elbadawi and S. Yeo (eds.) *Regional Integration and Trade Liberalization in SubSaharan Africa. Vol. 3: Regional Case Studies* (London: Macmillan).

Johnson, O. E. G. (1991) 'Economic Integration in Africa: Enhancing Prospects for Success', *Journal of Modern African Studies*, **29**.

Kaldor, N. (1970) 'The Case for Regional Policies', *Scottish Journal of Political Economy*, **17**(3).

Kasekende, L. A. and N. Ng'eno (1999) 'Regional Integration and Economic Liberalization in Eastern and Southern Africa' in A. Oyejide, I. Elbadawi and S. Yeo (eds.) *Regional Integration and Trade Liberalization in SubSaharan Africa. Vol. 3: Regional Case Studies* (London: Macmillan).

Krugman, P. (1981) 'Intra-industry Specialisation and the Gains from Trade', *Journal of Political Economy,* **89**.

Krugman, P. (1983) 'New Theories of Trade among Industrial Countries', *American Economic Review*, **73**.

Krugman, P. (1987) *Strategic Trade Policy and the New International Economics* (Cambridge, Mass.: MIT).

Krugman, P. (1993) *Integration, Specialization and Adjustment* (London: Centre for Economic Policy Research, Discussion Paper no. 886).

Krugman, P. (1994) 'Complexity and Emergent Structure in the International Economy', in Conference Report, *The Location of Economic Activity: New Theories and Evidence* (London: Centre for Economic Policy Research).

Landes, D. S. (1990) 'Why are We so Rich and They so Poor?' *American Economic Association Papers and Proceedings*, **80**(2).

Lyakurwa, W. 'Regional Integration and Trade Liberalization in SubSaharan Africa: Regional Case-Study of the SADC', AERC.

Lyakurwa, W., A. McKay, N. Ng'eno, W. Kennes (1997) 'Regional Integration in SubSaharan Africa: A Review of Experiences and Issues' in A. Oyejide, I. Elbadawi and P. Collier (eds.) *Regional Integration and Trade Liberalization in SubSaharan Africa. Vol. 1: Framework, Issues and Methodological Perspectives* (London: Macmillan).

Maasdorp, G. (1994) 'Models of Co-operation in Southern Africa', in M. Venter (ed.), *Prospects for Progress – Critical Choices for Southern Africa* (Cape Town: Maskew Miller Longman, 1994).

M'Bet, A. (1999) 'The CEAO and UEMOA within ECOWAS: The Road ahead towards West African Economic Integration' in A. Ojeyide, I. Elbadawi and S. Yeo (eds.) *Regional Integration and Trade Liberalization in SubSaharan Africa. Vol. 3: Regional Case Studies* (London: Macmillan).

McCarthy, C. (1992) 'The Southern African Customs Union in a Changing Economic and Political Environment', *Journal of World Trade*, **26**(4).

McCarthy, C. (1995) 'Regional Integration: Part of the Solution or Part of the Problem?', in S. Ellis (ed.) *Africa Now – People Policies Institutions* (London: James Currey and Heinemann).

Mistry, P. (1995) 'Open Regionalism: Stepping Stone or Milestone toward an Improved Multilateral System', in J. Teunissen (ed.), *Regionalism and the Global Economy – The Case of Latin America and the Caribbean* (The Hague: Forum on Debt and Development (Fondad)).

Mistry, P. (1996) 'Regional Dimensions of Structural Adjustment in Southern Africa', paper read at a Fondad Conference on *Regional Integration in Africa* (Johannesburg, February 1996).

Mortimer, R. (1993) 'Regionalism and Geopolitics in the Maghrib', *Middle East Report*, Sept.–Oct.

Mwase, N. and G. Maasdorp (1999) 'The Southern African Customs Union (SACU)' in A. Oyejide, I. Elbadawi and S. Yeo (eds.) *Regional Integration and Trade Liberalization in SubSaharan Africa. Vol. 3: Regional Case Studies* (London: Macmillan).

Myrdal, G. (1957) *Rich Lands and Poor* (New York: Harper & Row).

Mytelka, L. K. (1975) 'The Salience of Gains in Third-World Integrative Systems', *World Politics*, **25**.

National Economic and Social Council (1989) *Ireland in the European Community: Performance, Prospects and Strategy* (Dublin: NESC).

Ncube, M., P. Collier, K. Mlambo, and J. W. Gunning (1999) 'Zimbabwe' in Oyejide, A., B. Ndulu and J. W. Gunning (eds.) *Regional Integration and Trade Liberalization in SubSaharan African. Vol. 2: Country Case-Studies* (London: Macmillan).

O'Connell, S. A. (1997) 'Macroeconomic Harmonization, Trade Reform and Regional Trade in SubSaharan Africa' in A. Oyejide, I. Elbadawi and P. Collier (eds.) *Regional Integration and Trade Liberalization in SubSaharan Africa. Vol. 1: Framework, Issues and Methodological Perspectives* (London: Macmillan).

Okolo, J. E. (1990) 'The Development and Structure of ECOWAS', in J. E. Okolo and S. Wright (eds), *West African Regional Cooperation and Development* (Boulder, Colo.: Westview Press).

Onitiri, H. M. A. (1997) 'Changing Political and Economic Conditions for Regional Integration in SubSaharan Africa' in A. Oyejide, I. Elbadawi and P. Collier (eds.) *Regional Integration and Trade Liberalization in SubSaharan Africa. Vol. 1: Framework, Issues, and Methodological Perspectives* (London: Macmillan).

Ostergaard, T. (1993) 'Classical Models of Regional Integration – What Relevance for Southern Africa?', in B. OdÇn (ed.), *Southern Africa after Apartheid – Regional Integration and External Resources* (Nordiska Afrikainstitutet, 1993).

Ranis, G. (1995) 'Another Look at the East Asian Miracle', *World Bank Economic Review*, **9**(3).
Ravenhill, J. (1986) 'Collective Self-Reliance or Collective Self-Delusion: Is the Lagos Plan a Viable Alternative?' in J. Ravenhill (ed.) *Africa in Economic Crisis* (Basingstoke: Macmillan).
Rimmer, D. (1988) 'Africa's Economic Future', *African Affairs*.
Robson, P. (1988) 'The West African Economic Community', in A. M. El-Agraa (ed.), *International Economic Integration* (Basingstoke: Macmillan).
Trimble, M. J. (1990) 'The Impact of the European Community', in R. Harris, C. Jefferson and J. Spencer (eds), *The Northern Island Economy: A Comparative Study in the Economic Development of a Peripheral Region* (London: Longman).
World Trade Organization (1995) *Regionalism and the World Trading System* (Geneva).
World Bank, The (1991) *Intra-Regional Trade in Sub-Saharan Africa*, report no. 7685-AFR.
World Bank, The (1995) *World Development Report 1995* (Washington, DC).

3 SubSaharan Africa's Trade Liberalization Experience

Séamus O'Cléireacáin

3.1 INTRODUCTION

The importance of the country case-studies of this research project is evident when reviewing the coverage of the major multi-country trade liberalization case-studies of the past 25 years. The present project will serve to increase greatly African representation in such studies. The pioneering studies of Little, Scitovsky and Scott (1970) and Balassa (1971) contained no African representation. In Krueger's (1978) study of nine countries, Ghana was the only one from Africa. The Papageorgiou–Michaely–Choksi (1991) study of 19 countries had no African representative. Even in the recent literature combining economics with politics, the emphasis, to date, has been on Latin America and Eastern and Central Europe. The Nelson (1990) study includes one chapter on Africa in which Callaghy examines the politics of economic adjustment in Ghana, Zambia, and Nigeria. Not until Bates and Krueger (1992) did African representation in multi-country case studies begin to increase.

As the papers in the earlier volumes of this project indicate, Africa lags behind most other developing countries in the speed and durability of trade liberalization. There are no sustained 'big bang' stories among the case-study countries here. In most instances, the pace of change falls well short of that experienced in most of Latin America in recent years, never mind the speed of reform in Eastern Europe. In many of these other countries, economic reform has been accompanied by a vigorous political debate, an occurrence still lacking in many of the countries of this sample and a topic to which we shall return below. Latin America, the intellectual home of import-substitution development strategies, has, in most instances, moved rapidly to embrace trade liberalization as a policy goal.[1] Eastern and Central Europe is well on its way back to markets with trade liberalization as an element of that change. Asia is the home of the Asian Miracle (World Bank, 1993). None of these other parts of the world, of course, have renounced trade protection. However, they have moved to embrace the process of globalization and have sought to reduce the extent to which trade policy contains an anti-export bias.

There is considerable hope for the future to be found among the diversified experiences of the 10 country case-studies presented here, although the process of liberalization has been fitful. The experience has been, as might be expected, quite mixed. This chapter offers a comparative look at the trade liberalization experiences of the case-study countries by highlighting the experience with trade liberalization and economic reform generally in other developing countries and by examining the extent to which the case-study countries kept pace with changes elsewhere. It begins with some background data on basic trends for the 10 countries. This is followed by a broad treatment of the political economy of trade liberalization that draws heavily on political science literature and presents data on political and civil liberties trends as well as fiscal indicators of changing reliance on trade taxation. The implications of the failure to integrate more fully into the world economy are examined in a section on liberalization, openness and growth, while a section on African participation in the Uruguay Round presents some data on the extent to which this group of countries did, or did not, use the Round to consolidate domestic reforms. The final section attempts to draw some lessons from the East Asian experience prior to the crisis of 1997–8.

3.2 THE RECORD TO DATE

The ten countries that are the subjects of the case-studies are a highly dissimilar group. They include the two economic giants of subSaharan Africa (SSA), Nigeria and South Africa. Also included are some of their neighbours, which are attempting to pursue independent policies even as they contemplate further movement on economic integration. As Table 3.1 shows, the sample varies in per capita income from one of the poorest, Tanzania, with a 1993 GNP per capita of $110, to two of the richest, Mauritius and South Africa, at $2980 and $2902 respectively. GNP per capita is far below the levels of 10 or 15 years ago in six of the ten countries and has only shown dynamic growth in Mauritius and South Africa. Of the ten,

Table 3.1 African economic performance 1975–most recent

	Average per capita GNP ($)			*Average GDP growth p.a. ($)*	
	1975–9	*1980–5*	*1993*	*1980–5*	*1986–93*
SSA	489	635	483	1.3	1.8
Côte d'Ivorie	790	903	630	–1.4	–1.0
Ghana	332	377	430	–0.9	4.6
Kenya	296	372	270	2.8	3.7
Mauritius	980	1145	2980	2.6	6.4
Nigeria	758	1028	310	–2.7	5.0
South Africa	1514	2358	2902	1.9	0.9
Tanzania	212	300	110*	0.9	5.8
Uganda	–	153	190	–	5.1
Zambia	542	557	370	0.4	1.1
Zimbabwe	578	777	540	4.7	2.0

*1992 data.

Source: World Bank (1995) Tables 2–17 and 2–1.

all but Ghana, Mauritius, South Africa and Uganda had lower GNP per capita in 1993 than they had, on average, 1975–9. However, this is a group of countries whose growth performance since 1986 has, with few exceptions, vastly exceeded the average performance of SSA. Only one of them, Côte d'Ivoire, registered negative GDP growth in the period 1986–93, and only two others, South Africa and Zambia, registered GDP growth rates below the 1.8 per cent per annum average for SSA.

Between 1960 and 1990, the volume of world merchandise trade rose almost sixfold, outstripping the trebling of world merchandise that occurred over the same interval (GATT, 1995, p. 29). The differences in growth rates produced the burst in growing openness and interdependence of national economies with which we are all familiar. As Table 3.2 indicates, six of the ten countries in the sample did not participate in this almost universal trend and were less open in 1990 than they had been in 1960. For comparison purposes, Table 3.2 also contains the data for two Latin American and two Asian economies. The quantum leap in the openness ratios of these economies is worth observing. That of South Korea quadrupled from 16 per cent to 63 per cent, while that of Taiwan trebled from 30 per cent to 90 per cent. Argentina and Brazil, on the other hand, have more in common with much of Africa in this respect.

Table 3.2 Trends in per capita income and openness, 1960–94

	Real GDP per capita ($) (t/t adjusted)		*Openness*		*Year opened: Sachs–Warner criteria 1994*
	1960	*1990*	*1960*	*1990*	
Côte d'Ivoire	1101	1143	62	64	closed
Ghana	926	901	52	39	1985
Kenya	725	907	59	58	1993
Mauritius	2890	6012	69	142	independence
Nigeria	502	947	22	65	closed
S. Africa	2162	3244	57	47	1991
Tanzania	341	527*	64	63*	closed
Uganda	572	522	23	25	1988
Zambia	1207	672	93	70	1993
Zimbabwe	1188	1177	83	59	closed
S. Korea	899	6866	16	63	
Taiwan	1258	8211	30	90	
Argentina	4496	4663	18	15	
Brazil	1844	4029	12	13	

Notes: Real GDP per capita in constant dollars adjusted for changes in terms of trade. Openness ratio is (exports + imports) as a percentage of nominal GDP.
*Tanzania data are for 1988.

Sources: Penn World Table Mark 5.6 and Sachs and Warner, 1995. The Penn World Table data are downloadable from http:/www.nber.org/pwt56.html.

All ten countries covered in this project were included in the sample used by Sachs and Warner (1995) in their analysis of globalization and reform. They define a country as closed if it meets any one of five criteria: NTB coverage exceeding 40 per cent of imports; average nominal tariff rates exceeding 40 per cent; a differential of at least 20 per cent between the black market and official exchange rates; a Kornai-defined socialist economic system; or a state monopoly on major exports. Table 3.2 shows the state of the ten countries according to the Sachs-Warner criteria. Four of the ten countries, Côte d'Ivoire, Nigeria, Tanzania and Zimbabwe, were judged 'closed' as of 1994.

African countries largely sat out the Uruguay Round, and their regional integration efforts lack credibility. Now they watch Latin America countries join with North American Free Trade Agreement

(NAFTA) members to embrace the Miami Declaration goal of a hemispheric free trade area by 2010. At the same time, Asian countries adopt an Asia–Pacific Economic Community (APEC) goal of a free trade area by 2010 for its developed country members and 2020 for its developing country members. In Europe, the Commission of the European Union (EU) continues to push its members to implement fully the 1992 programme to complete its internal market even as it moves to extend trade liberalization by bringing the countries of Eastern Europe into its set of preferential arrangements.

All of these processes are incomplete. However, the contrast with common development strategies of 20 years ago is striking. Import substitution and hostility to foreign investment have been replaced by a lowering of barriers to both trade and capital flows, with, occasionally, even an unseemly scramble between developing countries competing to host direct foreign investment manufacturing projects of major multinational corporations. If the international financial network is the nervous system of the global economy, the rapid growth of so-called 'emerging financial markets' is a useful indicator of which developing countries appear to be furthest ahead of the curve on economic liberalization. To date, in mid-1996, there has been limited African participation. Of the $167 bn in net private capital flows to developing countries in 1995, less than $5 bn went to Africa.[2] Individual Latin American countries such as Argentina and Brazil each attracted more than the entire African continent.

3.3 THE POLITICAL ECONOMY OF AFRICAN TRADE LIBERALIZATION

The political environment within which economic agents operate undoubtedly influences the range of information available to them as well as the set of incentives and disincentives. Sustainable economic reform programmes require an enabling environment of stable, legal and political institutions where there is transparency and predictability in regulatory decision-making. As with much of Africa, the sample of countries is typified, in many cases, by severe restrictions on the political and civil liberties of economic agents. Several of the country studies refer to changes in the political environment within which economic policy is made and with which private agents must cope. South Africa is the most obvious recent example. It was also a consideration mentioned by the researchers examining the case of Zimbabwe, who refer to one-party rule, while a discussion of the first multi-party elections in Zambia in 1991 is included in the case-study for that country. The Zambian country study points to the manner in which the pace of reform accelerated after the election of the MMD government.

Table 3.3 contains the Freedom House indexes for political and civil liberties for the ten countries during the bulk of the years covered by the trade liberalization efforts examined in the case-studies. The indexes are based on a methodology that employs a checklist for both categories of freedom. Political rights indicators include whether the head of state/government was elected through what were adjudged to be free and fair elections, whether legislative representatives are similarly elected, whether there is freedom to organize political parties, and so on. The rating of civil liberties is conducted in a similar manner with concern for the existence of a free and independent media, open public discussion, freedom of assembly, equality under the law and access to an independent judiciary, free and independent trade unions, free religious expression, and absence of extreme corruption. Both ratings are calculated on a scale of 1–7, with a score of 7 being restricted for the most repressive societies.

As Table 3.3 indicates, by 1994, Mauritius, South Africa and Zambia had clearly distanced themselves from the more repressive countries in the sample on the issue of political rights. Mauritius and South Africa also stand out on the scale for civil liberties, with South Africa, of course, having made particular progress in recent years. At the other end of the spectrum, Kenya, Nigeria and Tanzania were listed as the most repressive members of the sample in 1994 on the civil liberties scale. As of 1994, the trend toward greater political and civil liberties was not yet fully apparent among the sample. Indeed, six of the ten had recently registered reductions in civil liberties.

Table 3.3 also underscores the recent trend toward founding elections that has accompanied economic reform efforts in many of the countries covered by this project. Founding elections are defined as those in which the office of head of government is openly contested after a period in which multi-party political competition was denied. Two of the ten countries, Mauritius and Zimbabwe, have regularly allowed competitive multi-party elections since before 1990. With the Tanzanian election of October 1995, all of the sample except Uganda had founding elections by the end of 1995, although,

Table 3.3 Political and civil liberties in Africa, 1975–95

Political rights/ civil liberties (scale: best to worst, 1–7)	*1975*	*1980*	*1985*	*1992*	*1994*	*Founding elections*	*Free and fair?*
Côte d'Ivoire							
Political rights	6	6	6	6	6	Oct. 1990	Yes?
Civil liberties	6	5	5	4	5		
Ghana							
Political rights	7	4	7	5	5	Nov. 1992	Yes?
Civil liberties	5	4	6	5	4		
Kenya							
Political rights	5	5	6	4	6	Dec. 1992	No
Civil liberties	4	4	5	5	6		
Mauritius							
Political rights	3	2	2	2	1	Regular	
Civil liberties	2	4	2	2	2		
Nigeria							
Political rights	6	2	7	5	7	Jun. 1993	No
Civil liberties	4	3	5	4	6		
S. Africa							
Political rights	4	5	5	5	2	Apr. 1994	Yes
Civil liberties	5	6	6	4	3		
Tanzania							
Political rights	6	6	6	6	6	Oct. 1995	Yes?
Civil liberties	6	6	6	5	6		
Uganda							
Political rights	7	6	5	6	5	No	
Civil liberties	7	6	4	5	5		
Zambia							
Political rights	5	5	5	2	3	Oct. 1991	Yes
Civil liberties	4	5	5	3	4		
Zimbabwe							
Political rights	6	4	4	5	5	Regular	
Civil liberties	5	5	6	4	5		

Sources: Political and civil liberties indicators from Freedom House, *Freedom in the World: The Annual Survey of Political Rights and Civil Liberties* (New York: Freedom House), various issues. Election indicators from Bratton and van de Walle (forthcoming).

as reported by Bratton and van de Walle (forthcoming), Kenya, and Nigeria had not yet had free and fair elections in recent history. Elsewhere in Africa, even with the recent movement toward political pluralism and multi-party politics with elected governments rather than one-party states and military juntas, there have been retrogressions. In early 1996, Niger's first democratically elected president was overthrown by a military *coup d'état* some weeks after a *coup d'état* in Sierra Leone on the eve of multi-party elections, while in mid-1996 aid donors suspended aid to Zambia in response to the government's policy of preventing ex-President Kaunda from standing for election.

Until fairly recently, much of the literature on the politics of economic reform had read the Latin American experience with military governments as one in which authoritarian governments were more likely to succeed in implementing unpopular economic reform measures. As Bates (1993) reminds us, however, much of the newest literature finds no strong relationship between political authoritarianism and economic reform. Bhagwati (1995, 1996) sees as implausible the notion that development requires authoritarian structures. For Bhagwati, the earlier, but in his view now defunct, claims in support of authoritarianism reflected the use of Harrod–Domar growth models and a stress on raising savings rates, particularly those of the public sector. Moreover, it may be argued that processes expand the choice set of individual responses to economic incentives, thus promoting growth, particularly in an endogenous growth framework rather than a Harrod–Domar setting.

In their empirical investigation of how governance structures influence the durability of economic reforms, Ball and Hauser (1995) conclude that an authoritarian government may be more successful in implementing unpopular inflation-reduction policies in the short run. Nevertheless they assert that such governments that, through greater openness and participation, allow a consensus to emerge in support of the objective. Although limited to inflation reduction, their results may also be applicable to other instances of reform such as those examined in these volumes. Trade liberalization is more an element of structural adjustment than stabilization. As Nelson (1990, p. 359) points out, it is likely to face determined long-term resistance from threatened interests and the liberalization may require phasing in over many stages. This is a common theme in many of the case-studies in the earlier volumes. In the early stages of industrialization, import-substitution interests are likely to have more political influence than an emerging export-orientated sector. The large role played by state-owned companies, which in other developing countries would be in private hands and be commercially-minded, ensures that this sector is not to be counted on as a supporter of reform in many African cases.

Most of the countries included in the case-studies could be described as 'soft' states, in the terms of Jones and Sakong (1980). They distinguish between 'hard' states that are capable of effectively steering the private sector's development, and 'soft' states where policies are subject to change by those who are the very objects of the policy. In soft states, policies end up generating rents rather than encouraging industrialization. As Rodrik (1992) argues, dictatorial regimes in SSA have often followed soft policies despite their authoritarian nature. For Rodrik, the existence of a soft state, and with it the likelihood that import-substitution development strategies will be subverted and transformed into rent-creating regimes, is a strong argument against pursuing a South Korean strategy of selective protection.

What may set the African countries of this study apart from the Asian and Latin American experience may be the emergence of what Callaghy (1990) sees as a post-independence pattern of both weak states and weak markets produced by a political economy of state cronyism fed by the introduction of market distortions and the extraction and distribution of rent to finance clientalist networks. In this pattern, the state is expanded, particularly through parastatals, state welfare services and subsidies are used to buy urban support, and control of foreign exchange is a vital component of the new political economy through which post-independence political elites maintain power.

Several of the country studies comment on the frequent and capricious changes that occur in trade policy. Complicated, arbitrary and non-transparent trade policy regimes provide obvious avenues for corruption. Wide tariff dispersion offers opportunities to create a market among customs officials in the misclassification of products as well as incentives for importers to misrepresent the nature of the product, thus undercutting the level of protection provided by the nominal tariff structure. Proposals for reducing or simplifying trade laws pose an obvious threat to all those whose income has been derived from policy-induced rent, including manipulation or evasion of trade laws.

Corruption is becoming a topic of much greater interest to development economists and to the world's media. The arrival of corruption-fighting NGOs such as Transparency International and the World Bank's new emphasis on the deleterious effects of corruption are likely to ensure that, for good or ill, national practices will come in for greater international attention and will have an influence on bilateral and multilateral aid flows. Four of the ten countries represented by country case-studies are included in the 1996 Transparency International rankings of perceived corruption in 54 developed and developing countries.[3] Using a composite index ranging from 0 (perceived to be totally corrupt) to 10 (perceived to be totally clean), the four that received ratings in 1996 were South Africa (a rating of 5.7, ranked 23rd), Uganda (2.7, ranked 43rd), Kenya (2.2, ranked 52nd) and Nigeria (0.7, ranked last). The country coverage of Transparency International's rankings is expanding rapidly and as it does, a larger number of African countries may be expected to be included.

The fiscal implications of trade liberalization are considerable for many of the countries in the sample. The individual country comparisons present a very mixed picture of the fiscal environment within which the trade policy examined in the case-studies has been conducted. Table 3.4 shows that all but Zambia registered prime fiscal deficits in 1993. The prime deficit for SSA in the years since 1986 has averaged 10 per cent. Four countries (Côte d'Ivoire, Ghana, South Africa and Uganda) ran larger deficits in 1993 than they had averaged in recent years. Five countries (Kenya, Mauritius, Nigeria, Tanzania and Zimbabwe) registered some reduction from past average deficits.

Table 3.4 indicates dependence on taxation of international trade and transactions as a source of revenue. The average SSA dependence on this source has averaged 15 per cent of non-grant government revenue. Of the ten, only South Africa and Tanzania have a lower reliance on this source of revenue while Mauritius, one of the most open of the ten economies in terms of trade-to-GDP ratios, has one of the highest dependencies on trade taxation as a source of revenue. Only three of the ten (Kenya, Mauritius and Nigeria) display a clear reduction in dependence on this tax base in the years since 1980. Table 3.4 suggests that only Ghana had a high dependence on export taxation, although Ssemogerere and Fielding (1999), in the Uganda case-study, mention that at an earlier period that country's coffee export duty financed 30–60 per cent of recurrent public spending. Of course, Table 3.4 does not indicate tax incidence

Table 3.4 Fiscal Indicators

	Government prime deficit/surplus % of GDP 1993	*Government prime deficit/surplus % of GDP 1986-most recent*	*Import duties as % of total non-grant revenue 1986-most recent*	*Export duties as % of total non-grant revenue 1986-most recent*	*Total taxes on international trade and transactions as % of total non-grant revenue 1975–79*	*Total taxes on international trade and transactions as % of total non-grant revenue 1980–85*	*Total taxes on international trade and transactions as % of total non-grant revenue 1986-most recent*
SSA	–9	–10	12.3	2.4	17.4	14.3	15.1
Côte d'Ivoire	–29	–15	27.2	7.5	. . .	35.6	35.2
Ghana	–11	–5	18.4	21.1	45.8	36.5	39.4
Kenya	–9	–10	16.2	1.4	20.3	21.3	17.6
Mauritius	–2	–4	39.9	6.8	41.9	49.1	47.1
Nigeria	–13	–15	11.4	0.1	16.6	15.5	15.7
S. Africa	–14	–9	3.6	0	5.8	3.5	5.2
Tanzania	–2*	–5	. . .	. . .	20.5	9.6	13.9
Uganda	–15	–8	. . .	. . .	52.4	53.4	62.9
Zambia	+5	–6	17.1	8.3	7.1	12.3	32.4
Zimbabwe	–10	–13	16.2	0	4.1	11.6	16.6

Notes: The prime surplus/deficit excludes interest payments on past debt. Total taxes on international trade and transactions include profits of government-controlled export or import monopolies, profits of monetary authorities on foreign exchange transactions, and taxes on the sale of foreign exchange.
*1992 data.

Source: The World Bank *African Development Indicators 1994–95* (Washington, DC: The World Bank, 1995) tables 7–3, 7–10, 7–11, 7–12.

and Tutu and Oduro (1999) refer, in the Ghana case-study, to the estimates of Jebuni *et al.* (1994) that up to 85 per cent of Ghanian import taxation is shifted to exports because of the high import content of exports. Bleaney *et al.*, in the South Africa case-study, mention a similar shift in incidence toward taxation of exports that occurred with the dismantling of South African quantitative restrictions.

In the absence of drastic curtailments in the role of the state, trade liberalization calls for alternative sources of tax revenue if fiscal deficits are not to widen. As a first step, according to Adam and Musonda, (1999) the authors of the Zambia case-study, relaxation of quantitative restrictions may shift the composition of imports toward consumer goods, which tend to have high tariff rates. A similar point is made by Neube *et al.* (1999) in the Zimbabwe case-study. However, the search for an expanded tax base faces difficulties in economies with large informal sectors. Muñoz (1994) describes Latin American instances in which tax reform and stronger enforcement more than compensated for lost tariff revenue. Taube and Tadesse (1996) advocate 'presumptive taxation' as a general strategy to expand the tax base and as an effort to reduce tax evasion, particularly in the informal sector. Presumptive income taxation might include presumptive import levies, business licence levies and withholding tax schemes.

In Taube and Tadesse's description, import taxes would be imposed, not as a form of protection but to capture some of the income presumed to be derived from the later sale of these imports. Neube *et al.* in the Zimbabwe case-study, describe the role of tariffs as revenue-raising rather than industry-protecting as long as a foreign exchange allocation scheme is the binding constraint on imports. Only with foreign exchange liberalization does the tariff structure become the principal source of protection. For Taube and Tadesse, presumptive taxes on imports would, in the case of registered taxpayers, be part payment of any general tax liability. In the case of the informal sector, they would become presumptive income taxes. However, schemes such as these require honest, competent administrative structures. As Adam and Musonda (1999) point out in the case-study of Zambia, prior to 1994, rebates were rarely paid in that country's customs duty drawback scheme due, in part, to weak administrative capacity. The schemes described by Taube and Tadesse would place even greater strains on a country's fiscal administrative machinery.

3.4 TRADE LIBERALIZATION, OPENNESS AND GROWTH

A follower of the literature on trade and endogenous growth would find worrisome any further continuation of the stagnant African openness ratios described earlier. In endogenous growth models such as those of Grossman and Helpman (1991), trade plays a role in promoting growth through its function as a mechanism to diffuse technological innovation. This mechanism is one in which imports are the growth promoters, although, as Richardson (1993) has shown, the importance of exports should not be underestimated either. Indeed, many of the country study papers discuss the anti-export bias of the past.

In his study of export disincentives in the United States, Richardson cited a range of reasons for paying greater attention to the microeconomic, efficiency-conducive characteristics of exports even in a large economy where the domestic market is big enough to yield scale economies. These include the self-insurance that occurs as a firm diversifies its customer base to include export markets, the jobs and income generated when export markets yield gainful employment for otherwise unemployed resources, the reduced need for import compression provided by the resulting flow of foreign exchange, and the economies in fixed costs when an export-enlarged customer base allows fixed resource costs to be spread more widely. Internal efficiencies may be expected to follow from having to face the intensified competition that rages in export markets. In addition, exports represent channels of information about foreign markets when early and sustained exports by some firms yield information externalities to others considering becoming export-orientated.

Frankel and Romer (1996) recently attempted to estimate the impact of trade on income by first using a gravity model to construct instruments for trade and then estimating a regression of income on trade and other variables. Even as they warn, in the preliminary version of their research, that there is considerable uncertainty in their estimates and that their results do not provide decisive support for the argument that trade improves income, their estimates suggest that a one-point increase in both export to GDP and import to GDP ratios would raise per capita income by two percentage points or more. Their results, however preliminary, provide a further inducement to getting African openness ratios moving in the same direction as the rest of the world.

For Sachs and Warner (1995), who make use of an interest-group political economy approach to economic policy formulation, the transition from closed to open economies should be faster in economies that are land-scarce and labour-abundant if governments are expected to be more responsive to labour than to landowners.

If, however, as Anders Aslund (Sachs and Warner, 1995, p. 98) holds, 'ideology and elites are more important than interest groups in countries with poor political structures', and if, as Sachs and Warner (1995, p. 57) hold, trade reform is part of the overall institutional harmonization with the advanced market economies', then political structures that permit if not encourage access to information and the free discussion of ideas may be more important in framing the environment within which trade policy is formulated. The role of international organizations and the obligations that come with membership should also not be underestimated. Participation in the WTO's Trade Policy Review Mechanism (TPRM), discussed below, is a useful example. However, Africa's past role in the GATT has been minimal in most instances. More active participation in the WTO, could prove a useful impetus to continuing reforms.

3.5 AFRICA AND THE WTO

External commitments are often a useful *deus ex machina* to which policy-makers can have recourse when attempting to ward off interest groups seeking to curtail reform. Until recently, the GATT and WTO, including the Uruguay Round, had limited African participation. South Africa was the obvious exception of an African country committed to participation in the Round. Prior to the Uruguay Round, only 20 of the 38 SSA GATT members had even lodged a tariff schedule with the GATT (Sorsa, 1995). Of the ten countries in our sample, Ghana, Kenya, Mauritius, Tanzania and Uganda did not have a tariff schedule registered with the GATT at the beginning of the Uruguay Round. It is thus not too surprising that there is limited discussion in the country and regional integration case-studies of the role of the GATT/WTO.

The initial analyses of the impact of the Round on Africa stressed the perceived negative effects rather than the more important benefits that would follow from the decision to wind down the Multi Fibre Agreement (MFA) or through the greater discipline imposed on developed country protectionism under the strengthened dispute settlement rules. Instead, the possibility of special compensation for participating in the Marrakesh conference provided a political motivation for studies that would show that Africa would be a net loser from the Round. Two concerns were the impact of reforms in developed country agricultural support programmes and the erosion of, for example, EU and GSP preferences caused by reductions in MFN tariffs. The agriculture agreement, by reducing agricultural export subsidies, reduces the implicit resource transfer to food-importing countries and would raise world prices for affected products. This latter effect would, of course, also provide an incentive to African producers to expand production and cut food imports.

As Table 3.5 indicates, South Africa was the only one of the ten sample countries to make an offer of tariff reduction during the Uruguay Round. The rest of the sample chose average tariff bindings that were usually a multiple of the existing applied rates. In most instances, little effort was made to extend the coverage of tariff bindings. Though six of the ten countries had come into the Round with no or almost no tariff bindings, all left with some level of bindings although eight out of the ten left with 90 per cent of their industrial tariffs unbound. Moreover, as Harrold (1995) states in his study of the impact of the Round on Africa, the choice of bindings so far above applied rates indicates a mercantilist approach to Uruguay Round negotiations.

It is not clear what future concessions African countries expect to receive from other WTO members in return for future reductions in their bindings, and, of course, such reductions will have no impact on resource allocation until they produce a fall in applied and effective rates. In taking a mercantilist path, African countries may have given up the opportunity to use Round participation as a mechanism to reinforce the credibility of existing reform efforts. Indeed, some may see the failure to participate more fully as a measure of that very credibility. Adoption of the mercantilist approach and continued use of high trade barriers also postpones the benefits to the domestic economy that might be expected to flow through unilateral trade liberalization.

One purpose of the Round was to introduce tariffication in agriculture. This will facilitate future negotiation on reduction in agricultural protection. Uruguay Round participants were required to bind 100 per cent of their tariff lines in agriculture if they had not done so already, and to introduce a phased 36 per cent cut that was to occur over ten years for developing countries but from

Table 3.5 Participation in the Uruguay Round – selected indicators

	Agriculture		*Industry*			
	Tariff binding average rate	*Applied tariff average rate*	*Pre-round: % tariff lines bound*	*In round: % tariff lines bound*	*Tariff binding average rate*	*Applied tariff average rate*
Côte d'Ivoire	215	20	29.0	0.4	257	–
Ghana	98	22	0.0	1.1	33	16
Kenya	100	44	0.0	1.6	54	35
Mauritius	135	52	0.0	1.6	82	–
Nigeria	230	47	0.1	7.0	128	36
S. Africa	40	7	31.0	68.0	17	22
Tanzania	240	–	0.0	0.1	240	–
Uganda	80	–	0.0	2.7	50	–
Zambia	124	–	–	4.0	42	–
Zimbabwe	161	24	8.0	0.8	66	31

Sources: Harrold, 1995; Sorsa, 1995.

which the least-developed countries were exempt. While average applied rates are well below bound levels, a number of the countries in our sample registered agricultural duty bindings approaching or exceeding 100 per cent. South Africa and some members of SACU were clear exceptions to this pattern as these countries used the Round, to some extent, to bolster ongoing reform programmes.

Tariff bindings lock in progress on the domestic front and are useful in warding off lobbies seeking further protection. Internationally registered bindings become a way of importing credibility for a trade reform programme. In manufactures, most SSA countries bound less than 2 per cent of their tariff lines and of these, the average level of bindings frequently exceeded 100 per cent. This is a risible level, though not to be confused with applied rates.

The high level of bindings to which the Uruguay Round reductions will be applied will, in most African cases, leave post-cut bindings well above applied rates. Consequently, there will be no reduction in trade protection. Increasingly, as average tariffs on manufactures in developed countries have dwindled toward zero over the years, the attention of the main trading countries has moved to strengthening rules on contingent protection, dispute resolution and non-tariff barriers and, more recently, an emphasis on a sectoral approach in, for example, financial services, telecommunications and maritime services. To the extent that African governments rely on tariff protection not just to protect domestic industry and to allow the accumulation and distribution of rents to political supporters but as an important source of budget revenue, there may be little commonality of interest between African trade negotiators and the main participants in future multilateral trade negotiations. This was already particularly apparent in the Uruguay Round agricultural agreement, which, apart from its market access provisions, limited the extent to which developed countries subsidize agriculture including agricultural exports, something many African countries tax.

The Uruguay Round represented a major failure for African countries to shore up credibility in economic reform. Indeed, it should be taken as a danger signal that, in negotiations aimed at reciprocally increasing market access, so little was asked of African participants by other participants in the Round. The Round had offered the opportunity to lock in reform on the trade front in a manner similar to that presented by other international agreements such as the North American Free Trade Agreement (NAFTA), which locks in the domestic economic reforms under way in Mexico since the obligations of NAFTA membership are inconsistent with rolling back the trade policy reforms introduced by Mexico.

There is no need to wait until, if ever, there is a successor Round. A further mechanism to build credibility for trade liberalization measures is participation in the Trade Policy Review Mechanism (TPRM) of the World Trade Organization (WTO). Introduced in 1989 as part of the Mid-term Review Agreement of the Uruguay Round, the TPRM has three purposes: (1) improving adherence to WTO rules; (2) fostering greater transparency in country trade policies; and (3) permitting collective evaluations of each member's policies. For developing country WTO members, TPRM reviews are conducted once every six years or less frequently. As late as March 1996, of the 40 developing and transitional economies for which TPRM reports had been completed since the inception of the process in 1989, the only African countries were Cameroon, Côte d'Ivoire, Ghana, Kenya, Mauritius, Nigeria, Senegal, South Africa, Uganda and Zimbabwe. Eight of these are among the ten country case-studies. All but Tanzania and Zambia had completed the TPRM process.

Participation in the TPRM provides a useful discipline in several respects. Qureshi (1995) sees the process as having the potential to influence the conduct of members under review and, particularly for developing countries, to produce a heightened consciousness of the need for compatibility between domestic policies and international obligations. A TPRM review represents an organized inventory and evaluation of a WTO member's trade policy and provides a base line of transparency.[4]

This may go some way to alleviate a concern voiced in several of the country studies at the way in which tariff rates can vary arbitrarily and frequently. However, considerable latitude for capricious treatment of the taxation of imports will continue until tariff dispersion is reduced and tariff bindings are brought down to the level of effective tariff rates. To some degree, it may even be seen as a counterpart to the new effort at the IMF to establish a data base of financial indicators in the wake of the peso crisis of late 1994.

3.6 CAN AFRICA CATCH UP?

In their recent survey of economic reform and global integration, Sachs and Warner (1995) apply a very simple classification of inward and outward development strategies. In explaining the timing of liberalization they find two factors that appear significant in encouraging early liberalization – a high labour–land ratio and a high per capita income. They also report that from 1970 to 1989, open economies grew faster than closed economies and poor open economies grew faster than rich ones. In a result pregnant with implications for many African countries, they find that the process of convergence does not extend to closed economies. They also find that the shift from reliance on primary product production to manufacturing occurs faster in open than in closed economies and that the vulnerability to financial and inflation crises is greater for closed than for open economies.

The empirical literature on the link between trade liberalization and economic growth continues to produce mixed results. The notion that autarky or import substitution leads to failure and export-led growth strategies leads to success presents a very stark view of choices, which are usually more complicated in the messy world in which policy is made. Even as a growing number of countries move away from import substitution policies, Rodrik (1995) reminds us that some of the Asian NICs held up as role models for others have been countries in which there had been considerable state intervention. Indeed, in the cases of South Korea and Taiwan, these countries were launched on to high growth paths *before* exports became a substantial force in their economies. In Rodrik's reading of the success of South Korea and Taiwan, industrial policy from the 1950s onward overcame co-ordination failures caused by bureaucratic tangles and limited access to imported intermediate goods, but did so in an environment characterized by a relatively egalitarian income distribution and a lot of human capital.

For Rodrik, one of the key features of the Asian experience was government intervention through subsidies, public ownership and administrative guidance that created a climate for private enterprise and an increased private return to capital. Rodrik sees the export orientation *per se* as an insufficient explanation of the Asian success story. Instead of seeing exports as the source of growth in these countries, Rodrik points to the profitability of investment, with an investment boom sparking both an import and export boom. This reasoning reverses the causality between growth and exports. It is worth mentioning, in this regard, the view expressed by Ndulu, Semboja and Mbelle, in the Tanzania case-study, that in a foreign exchange-constrained economy, any reduction in import compression and enhanced availability of basic goods may have a bigger effect on production and investment than on exports. Ndulu *et al.* (1999) point to the 1984 own-funded import scheme, which boosted production growth *prior* to the intensive Tanzanian liberalization aimed at exports.

There is also, as Rodrik (1996) argues, the need to distinguish between unsustainable macroeconomic policies pursued by import-substituting countries and the effects of trade restrictions. As he reminds us, the failures of countries pursuing import-substitution strategies may have been due more to unsustainable macroeconomic policies or bureaucratic and institutional shortcomings than to microeconomic misallocation caused by trade policies. In those instances in which countries pursuing import-substitution development strategies have failed to make adequate progress, the causes of these failures need to dissected into, at minimum, those due to unsustainable populist macroeconomics and overinflated exchange rates and those due to the resource allocation effects of an import-substitution trade and industrial policy.

In seeking to understand why seemingly dysfunctional policies, such as import-substitution strategies and economic populism, have suddenly been discarded in so many countries simultaneously, Rodrik believes that the new orthodoxy of fiscal rectitude, competitive exchange rates, privatization, undistorted market prices and (with the exception of education and infrastructure) limited state intervention has misread some of the lessons of the East Asian success story. This has occurred even as the export-orientated strategy of these countries belied the export pessimism on which so much of the import-substitution strategy was based. Rodrik reminds us that Young (1994) and others have shown the miracle to be based on input growth – physical and human capital increases – rather than growth in total factor productivity.

In explaining why the Asian interventionist model was so successful while interventionist efforts elsewhere have failed, Rodrik points to the importance of such initial conditions as high human capital endowments relative to per capita income and relatively egalitarian income distribution. A simple regression of education on income for the ten countries included in the case-studies of this project would suggest that, for these countries, Ghana, Zimbabwe and Zambia are closest to meeting the first of these two initial conditions while Tanzania would appear to be furthest away.[10] On the income distribution front, a notoriously difficult phenomenon to measure, the share of total income or consumption going to the richest 10 per cent of the population may be used as an indicator of one point on the distribution. On this measure, the latest figure for South Korea is 27 per cent. Only Uganda (27 per cent), Côte d'Ivoire and Ghana (29 per cent each) report percentages in this range, while Kenya, South Africa, Tanzania and Zimbabwe all report percentages in the 47–48 per cent range (World Bank, 1995).

This admittedly simple empirical snapshot would suggest that none of the countries in the present sample yet possess both of the initial conditions identified by Rodrik as so important in producing a successful Asian-style interventionist export-orientated growth experience.

Trade liberalization is but one component in adjustment. Killick (1995) states that over the past 15 years, African economies have found it more difficult to adjust than have economies elsewhere. Elbadawi *et al.* (1992) had reached a similar conclusion. In his effort to examine the flexibility of economies, Killick distinguished between responsive and innovative flexibility. In a world of change there is a need to respond to change and also a need to drive change. Individuals, firms and institutions must possess responsive flexibility to react to changes in relative incentives. They must also possess innovative flexibility to initiate change. In the case of Africa, Killick argues that the response of economic agents to incentives shows

Africa to be as adaptive as elsewhere but that constraints on people ensure that the adaptiveness of enterprising people is not translated into flexible economies.

On the trade front, Killick (1995, pp. 159–60) points to the slow growth in export earnings, slow diversification toward manufactures and the slow diversification of export destinations. He notes three aspects of inflexibility in African economies. These are: (1) limited ability to take advantage of opportunities presented by the changed structure of world demand in international trade; (2) limited incorporation of technology into production; and (3) low supply elasticities. Echoing Rodrik, Killick (p. 175) does not blame excessive state intervention, but the wrong kind of intervention. While the same policy mistakes were often made in Latin American and Asian countries, African governments were slower to respond to the negative consequences of their dysfunctional policies because, in many instances, the primary function of government was to provide personal benefits or reward supporters rather than support development.

3.7 CONCLUSION

The papers of this project have tracked a faltering but continuing, episodic process toward a more rational trade policy in Africa. The country case-studies have clearly pointed to the progress on the macroeconomic and exchange rate front occurring in so many of the countries in the sample. There may have been more progress in removing exchange rate premiums than in achieving sustainable fiscal positions. Sustainable macroeconomic and exchange rate policies are a prerequisite to a successful trade policy even if, as Rodrik (1996) points out, that policy is an interventionist one.

As the case-studies indicate, African development policies are heavily interventionist. In evaluating East Asian miracle countries such as South Korea and Taiwan against John Williamson's list of the elements of the Washington Consensus, Rodrik finds the Asian countries adhering to the macroeconomic elements of the Consensus such as fiscal stringency, unified and competitive exchange rates, and so on, but diverging sharply from the Consensus in matters of microeconomic intervention. However, the East Asian form of intervention appears to have avoided rent-seeking activities; instead, it has promoted accumulation. In the African context, implementation of prescriptions such as those of Bates (1993), calling for the empowerment of technocrats and the creation of powerful economic bureaucracies that can institutionalize reform would represent a major departure from present practice in most instances.

Notes

1. Edwards (1993, p. 1370) remarks on the 'clear sense of déja vu' experienced in reading the rhetoric of the OAU's 1980 Lagos Plan of Action, which drew heavily on Latin American *dependencia theory.*
2. World Bank Debtor Reporting System.
3. Transparency International's perceived corruption rankings may be downloaded from http.\\www.gwdg.de/~uwvw/icr.htm.
4. Summaries of TPRM reports may be downloaded from the WTO's home page at http://www.WTO.org/WTO/reviews/reviews.htm.
5. An OLS equation on per capita GDP was estimated for the ten-country sample using terms-of-trade adjusted real per capita GDP as the income variable and percentage of age cohort enrolled in secondary education as the human capital variable. The results (available from the author) show that Ghana, Zimbabwe and Zambia have observed enrolments most above predicted values while Tanzania has a level furthest below predicted levels. Data sources: Penn World Bank Table Mark 5.6 and *World Bank Development Report 1995.*

References

Balassa, B. (1971) *The Structure of Protection in Developing Countries* (Baltimore: Johns Hopkins University Press).

Ball, R. and G. Hauser (1995) 'Governance Structures and the Durability of Economic Reforms: Evidence from Inflation Stabilizations', *World Development*, **23** (6): 897–912.

Bates, R. H. (1993) 'The Politics of Economic Policy Reform: a Review Article', *Journal of African Economies*, **2** (3): 417–33.

Bates, R. H. and A. O. Krueger (1992) *Politican and Economic Interactions in Economic Policy Reform* (Oxford: Blackwell).

Bhagwati, H. (1995) 'Democracy and Development: New Thinking on an Old Question', *Indian Economic Review*, **30** (1).

Bhagwati, J. (1996) 'The Global Age: from a Skeptical South to a Fearful North', Raul Prebisch Lecture at UNCTAD IX, Johannesburg, 29 April.

Bratton, M. and N. van de Walle (forthcoming) *Democratic Experiments in Africa: Regime Transitions in Comparative Perspectives* (Cambridge University Press).

Callaghy, T. M. (1990) 'Lost between State and Market: the Politics of Economic Adjustment in Ghana, Zambia and Nigeria', in J. Nelson, *Economic Crisis and Policy Choice* (Princeton University Press), 257–320.

Edwards, S. (1993) 'Openness, Trade Liberalisation and Growth in Developing Countries', *Journal of Economic Literature* **31**:1358–93.

Elbadawi, I. A., D. Ghura and G. Uwujaren (1992) 'Why Structural Adjustment has not Succeeded in Sub-Saharan Africa', *World Bank Working Paper* WPS 1001.

Frankel, J. A. and D. Romer (1996) 'Trade and Growth: an Empirical Investigation', NBER Working Paper no. 5476 (March).

GATT (1995) *International Trade: Trends and Statistics 1995* (Geneva: GATT).

Grossman, G. and E. Helpman (1991) *Innovation and Growth in the World Economy* (Cambridge, Mass.: MIT Press).

Harrold, P. (1995) 'The Impact of the Uruguay Round on Africa', *World Bank Discussion Papers*, 311 (November).

Jebuni, C. D., A. D. Oduro and K. A. Tutu (1994) *Trade, Payments Regime and Economic Performance in Ghana*, AERC Research Report no. 27 (Nairobi).

Jones, L. and I. Sakong (1980) *Government, Business and Entrepreneurship in Economic Development: The Korean Case* (Cambridge, Mass.: Harvard University Press).

Killick, Tony (ed.) (1995) *The Flexible Economy* (London: Routledge).

Krueger, A. O. (1978) *Foreign Trade Regimes and Economic Development: Liberalization Attempts and Consequences* (Cambridge: Ballinger for NBER).

Little, I., T. Scitovsky and M. Scott (1970) *Industry and Trade in Some Developing Countries* (Oxford University Press).

Muñoz, O. (1994) 'Towards Trade Opening: Legacies and Current Strategies', in J. M. Nelson *et al.*, *Intricate links: Democratization and Market Reforms in Latin America and Eastern Europe* (Washington DC: Overseas Development Council) pp. 61–104.

Ncube, M., P. Collier, K. Mlambo and J.W. Gunning (1999) 'Zimbabwe' in A. Oyejide, B. Ndulu and J.W. Gunning (eds) *Regional Integration and Trade Liberalization in SubSaharan Africa. Vol. 2: Country Case-Studies* (London: Macmillan) forthcoming.

Ndulu, B., J. Semboja and A.V.Y. Mbelle (1999) 'Tanzania' in Oyejide, A., B. Ndulu and J. W. Gunning (eds.) *Regional Integration and Trade Liberalization in SubSaharan Africa. Vol. 2: Country Case-Studies* (London: Macmillan) forthcoming.

Nelson, J. M. (1990) *Economic Crisis and Policy Choice* (Princeton University Press).

Nelson, J. M. *et al.* (1994) *Intricate Links: Democratization and Market Reforms in Latin America and Eastern Europe* (Washington DC: Overseas Development Council) pp. 61–104.

Papageorgiou, D., M. Michaely and A. M. Choksi (eds) (1991) *Liberalizing Foreign Trade* (Oxford: Blackwell).

Qureshi, A. H. (1995) 'Some Lessons from "Developing Countries": Trade Policy Reviews in the GATT framework – an enforcement perspective', *The World Economy*, **18** (3): 489–504.

Richardson, D. (1993) *Sizing up US Export Disincentives* (Washington DC: Institute for International Economics).

Rodrik, D. (1992) 'Conceptual Issues in the Design of Trade Policy for Industrialization', *World Development*, **20** (3): 309–20.
Rodrik, D. (1995) 'Getting Interventions Right: How South Korea and Taiwan Grew Rich', *Economic Policy*, 20 (April): 53–108.
Rodrik, D. (1996) 'Understanding Economic Policy Reform', *Journal of Economic Literature* **34** (March): 9–41.
Sachs, J. D. and A. Warner (1995) 'Economic Reform and the Process of Global Integration', *Brookings Papers on Economic Activity*, 1: 1–118.
Sorsa, P. (1995) 'The Uruguay Round and Sub-Saharan Africa's trade policies', mimeo (August).
Ssemogerere, G. and D. Fielding (1999) 'Uganda' in Oyejide, A., B. Ndulu and J. W. Gunning (eds.) *Regional Integration and Trade Liberalization in SubSaharan Africa. Vol. 2: Country Case-Studies* (London: Macmillan) forthcoming.
Taube, G. and H. Tadesse (1996) 'Presumptive Taxation in Sub-Saharan Africa: Experiences and Prospects', *IMF Working Paper*, no. 96/5.
Tutu, K. and A. Oduro (1999) 'Ghana' in Oyejide, A., B. Ndulu and J. W. Gunning (eds.) *Regional Integration and Trade Liberalization in SubSaharan Africa. Vol. 2: Country Case-Studies* (London: Macmillan) forthcoming.
World Bank, The (1993) *The East Asian Miracle* (Washington: The World Bank).
World Bank, The (1995) *World Development Report 1995*, pp. 220–1.
Young, A. (1994) 'Lessons from the East Asian NICs: a Contrarian View', *European Economic Review*, **38** (3, 4): 964–73.

4 Restraint, Co-operation and Conditionality in African Trade Policy

Paul Collier and Jan Willem Gunning

4.1 INTRODUCTION

There are various circumstances in which a government can gain by imposing restraints on its own behavior. The rational government, where it can construct such restraints, will therefore choose to do so. Section 4.2 presents a variety of situations in which the introduction of restraints actually relaxes a binding constraint. Section 4.3 argues that the history of African economic policy is characterized by a lack of restraints and that failure of private investment to recover despite the implementation of policy reforms is evidence that the shortage of restraints is costly. However, African governments are not in a position to create viable domestic agencies of restraint. The history of government abuse of power paradoxically curtails the power of governments to bind themselves. Hence, if African governments are to benefit from agencies of restraint, these agencies can only be external.

Section 4.4 analyses donor conditions as an attempt to turn aid into an external agency of restraint. It concludes that donor conditions have failed as an agency of restraint because of design flaws and that, given this history of failure, they cannot in the near future form the basis for credible restraint. Section 4.5 turns to the alternative of external agencies of restraint based on inter-governmental reciprocal threats. It argues that such institutions have been the preferred restraint mechanism of other governments and that they have been mistakenly ignored by African governments. Section 4.6 sets the scene for our application of this analysis to trade policy by reviewing the experience with regional integration. Section 4.7 then discusses the lock-in argument and the role Europe can play in providing an anchor for African regional groups. We argue that linking African regional groups to Europe through free trade agreements would provide credible penalties on policy reversal. Indeed, this is part of the rationale for the European Mediterranean Economic Area. Section 4.8 concludes.

4.2 RESTRAINTS THAT RELAX CONSTRAINTS

There are various circumstances in which a government might choose to impose restraints upon its own behaviour if only it is able to do so. We review six such circumstances, all of which are pertinent to African governments.

Time Consistency

In the African context, nearly half of government revenue has traditionally derived from trade taxes, the true incidence of which falls largely on the export sector. The African export sector is usually characterized by very long-lasting investment, the export being either a tree crop or mineral extraction. In these circumstances the export sector must take a long-run view of taxation and may conclude that regardless of promises to the contrary, the government will, should the export sector invest, rationally adopt a high taxation strategy. If the government should attempt to signal an intention to lower future taxation by adopting low current taxation, then the rational strategy for the export sector is not to invest but rather to bring forward future output to the present, whether by accelerated extraction in the case of minerals, or fertilizer in the case of tree crops. The attempt to attain the first best, namely private investment in the export sector, thereby achieves the third best, the diversion of resources into tax avoidance. The government is constrained because it cannot restrain itself.

The Rotten Descendant Problem

The better the government, the more forward-looking it is. The more forward-looking it is, the more it will fear the 'rotten descendant'. We illustrate this problem with reference to the European aristocracy. Typically, these households wished to perpetuate a dynasty in which the assets would be handed on intact generation to generation. The danger was that with unrestricted property rights one future generation would be rotten and so would consume the assets. The paradox would then be that the one generation that did not share the preferences of the present generation, and of which the present generation would therefore disapprove, would benefit most from the inheritance. If the risk of this was sufficiently high the very act of founding a dynasty by bequest was not worth while, since it amounted to a transfer from a good generation to a rotten one.

By the same reasoning, a prudent government can be constrained in its acts of prudence by the fear, not that its successor governments will in general be worse, but that a single rotten government, which we might think of as populist, will occur within the foreseeable future. The government is constrained because it cannot restrain future governments. An arrangement that restrained the future rotten government would relax a constraint upon the prudential behaviour of the present government without making the future rotten government worse off, since without the restraint there would be no inheritance for it to squander.

Endogenous Rotten Descendants

In the time-consistency problem above, a 'rotten' government with a preference for high taxation nevertheless had an interest in restraining itself because its future behaviour was endogenous to current private investment. In the second example, a 'good' government had an interest in restraining a future exogenously occurring 'rotten' government. Now the prospects of a future 'rotten' government are endogenized. Suppose that fiscal policy is the outcome of a contest between a highly conservative ministry of finance and extremely populist spending ministries. Each side puts forward a plan and the president chooses between them. Initially, the government has zero foreign assets so that the large fiscal deficit demanded by the spending ministries causes high inflation. The president therefore sides with the plan of the ministry of finance for a fiscal surplus. Each time he does this, reserves accumulate and so the inflationary consequences of the fiscal deficit plan diminish. Eventually, the inflation costs are sufficiently low that the president switches to populism. Anticipating this, the shrewd ministry is constrained to argue only for fiscal balance, since the accumulation of a prudential surplus would generate the 'rotten' government it opposes.

The Signalling Problem

Especially in the context of aided reform programmes, the mere act of reform cannot be taken at face value. It may be motivated by a desire to gain the aid, or to get debt rescheduling, after which the reform can be reversed. Not knowing the intentions of the government, the private sector cannot tell whether the government is genuine or not. Lacking full credibility, the reform will achieve only a reduced supply response and might indeed generate welfare-reducing speculation as analysed by Calvo (1988). The government is constrained because it cannot restrain itself. As Rodrik (1989a, b) has discussed in the context of trade policy, one solution to this problem is for the genuine reformer to undertake stronger reforms than it would otherwise choose. By making a reform that the non-genuine government would not choose to follow (because it perceives the costs of reform to be greater than does the genuine reformer) it can create a separating equilibrium. A second solution is for it to forgo the aid, so that were it a non-genuine government it would have no incentive to reform. However, if the genuine government is able to do so, its preferred option would be to enter a lock-in mechanism that prevents policy reversal by making it very costly. This achieves the same signal, since again it is something the non-genuine government would not be prepared to do, but without the cost 'excessive' reform.

The Endogenous Policy Problem

In some spheres of economic policy the policy changes in a predictable way. For example, as Schuknecht (1994) has shown, on average developing countries experience a political business cycle in which the fiscal deficit increases in the year of an election. Similarly, many African governments have adopted an endogenous trade policy (Collier and Gunning, 1995a, b; 1998) whereby trade restrictions are used to maintain balance of payments equilibrium in the face of temporary external shocks. A government that adopts these policy rules will reduce the fiscal deficit in the year after an election and will liberalize trade during a commodity boom. These changes will not be seen as permanent. Suppose, however, that in just these circumstances the government wishes to change the policy rule, whether to a permanently lower fiscal deficit or to a permanently more liberalized trade regime. The private sector cannot now distinguish between an application of the existing policy rule and a change in the rule. This creates a particularly severe signalling problem, since neither of the solutions suggested above (forgoing aid or excessive reform) are applicable. Further, it is liable to be a common problem in Africa; the government is most likely to be willing to change the fiscal policy rule after an election, and is most likely to want to change the trade policy rule at a time when the balance of payments is strong. The government is constrained because it cannot restrain itself; only the creation of locking-in mechanisms will permit reform to be credible at such times.

The Poor Reputation Problem

In Tirole's model of corruption the reputation of other agents regarded as similar is a potential asset or liability. Not knowing whether the particular individual is honest or not, other agents will partly infer likely behaviour from that of the other similar-seeming agents. If other similar agents are mostly honest, the unknown agent starts with the asset of the benefit of the doubt. It is, then, worth while to maintain this asset by behaving honestly. Conversely, if born into a dishonest society, the unknown agent starts with the liability of a presumed dishonesty, and given this presumption it may never be worth while to invest in the acquisition of an honest reputation. This analysis of hysteresis in corruption may equally be applied to the behaviour of an African government. Given that its predecessors have adopted poor policies and that its neighbours are also adopting poor policies, it may simply not be worth while to invest in the acquisition of a good reputation. The government would adopt good policies if only these were credible, but since they will not become credible for many years, it is not worth the investment. Again the government is constrained because it cannot restrain itself.

In each of these six cases the government can relax a binding constraint by introducing a non-binding constraint. That is, by restraining itself from actions it would in any case not choose to do, it can attain a previously unattainable outcome. The problem is one of designing credible penalties that would be exacted in the event of the undesired behaviour. The institutions that constitute these penalty systems we term *agencies of restraint.* These agencies can be either domestic or external. In each case the government chooses to adopt the restraint. However, whereas with a domestic agency the institution is entirely within the jurisdiction of the government, with an external agency the institution is beyond the government's jurisdiction.

4.3 DOMESTIC AGENCIES OF RESTRAINT IN AFRICA

In Africa prior to independence there could be no domestic agencies of restraint. The colonial authorities, being domestically all-powerful, were unable to restrain themselves. The colonial government was, however, itself subject to an imperial government that acted as an external agency of restraint. Upon independence, this agency was by definition removed, and so newly independent governments found themselves without restraints other than those provided by past habits. As one of us has previously argued (Collier, 1991), these habits were tested often during the shocks of the 1970s. Over a range of important economic policies – trade restrictions, the fiscal deficit, property rights, taxation – choices were made that were populist in that they extracted a short-term political advantage for a long-term economic cost. The power of African governments to adopt populist policies was often extraordinary by international standards. Wide-ranging quantitative import controls, often operating with firm specificity, were introduced at a time when elsewhere in the world trade restrictions were being reduced. Deficit financing, though not of Latin American proportions, produced triple-digit inflation in Ghana, Uganda, Zaire and Angola from a base of price stability. A wide range of commercial, mining and residential property was nationalized, sometimes without compensation. Implicit and explicit taxation of exports often rose to penal levels. Only a minority of governments adopted such extreme policies, but the fact that some chose to do so and that these choices were unrestrained, changed the nature of the uncertainties confronting both foreign and domestic investors. Instead of simply facing a set of commercial risks with known probabilities, agents faced Knightean uncertainty over a wide range of states of the world that had previously been dismissable. As Aizenman (1997) shows, the introduction of uncertainty can create much stronger deterrents to private investment than risk.

Although many of the most egregious economic policies adopted by African governments during the period 1970–90 have recently been reversed, private investment, both foreign and domestic, has remained at very low levels. For example, Africa has almost completely missed out on the enormous increase in foreign direct and portfolio investment into developing countries. The low level of private investment is arguably currently the single most serious weakness of African adjustment attempts, directly reducing both aggregate growth and the capacity of the economy to reallocate resources to export activities. Given the history of economic policy, investors might reasonably have concluded that periodically African governments have a preference for populism and that Africa lacks effective agencies of restraint so that these preferences get implemented. Uncertainty about future economic policy, and in particular the non-dismissability of highly disadvantageous scenarios, can powerfully discourage investment despite current policy reform. Recent survey evidence of the attitudes of foreign actual and potential investors to Africa (World Bank, 1994) supports this explanation for low investment. The survey found that the single most important deterrent to investment was the fear of policy reversal, inconvertibility and confiscation, this being more important than any current policy parameters such as regulation, taxation and infrastructure. Usually, foreign firms are better protected than domestic firms because they have resort to the leverage of their national governments. Hence, it is likely that the fears that discourage foreign investment also apply to domestic investment.

An implication of this is that Africa is currently paying a high price for its lack of agencies of restraint. Given its history, Africa more than other continents needs institutions that convincingly preclude disastrous policy scenarios. We now consider whether it is feasible for African governments themselves to construct domestic agencies of restraint.

Across independent Africa power has been very heavily concentrated in the presidency. Just as a domestically all-powerful colonial authority logically could not construct domestic agencies of restraint, and so depended upon external restraint, so with a domestically all-powerful president. The historical lack of domestic agencies of restraint in independent Africa is therefore a logical by-product of the form of government. However, during the 1990s there has been considerable democratization and this may appear to empower those governments that wish to construct domestic agencies of restraint.

In those countries that democratize on the British political model, democracy does not really provide this empowerment. Within British-style parliamentary democracy it is difficult to construct agencies that are legally proof against a determined government because this would conflict with the bedrock constitutional concept of the sovereignty of the current parliament, which in practice amounts to the sovereignty of the current government. The American system is better suited to legal limitations on the current government. However, in Africa the fundamental current problem is not that most countries are adopting a political system that is constitutionally ill-suited to the creation of domestic agencies of restraint, but that the notion that a government should be subject to the rule of law is recent and fragile. Most African governments have a history of overriding the rule of law when they found it expedient to do so. Until there is confidence in the rule of law, domestic agencies of restraint will not be credible. The notion that presidents and ministers may not exceed clearly circumscribed powers is alien to African experience and may take the next quarter century to establish. Until then, a president who wishes to restrain his powers in order to relax a binding constraint cannot do so by means of domestic agencies. In particular, consider the history of those ministers brave enough to oppose the wishes of their presidents. In many African countries ministers in this position have met with fatal accidents. With this legacy, regardless of the legal position, the head of an agency of restraint is unlikely to persist in an independent line. In practice, acts of individual courage may gradually change this expectation, but given the expectation, domestic agencies of restraint are currently ineffective at extricating a good government from its problem.

Indeed, in present African circumstances, the creation of domestic agencies of restraint encounters many of the problems set out above. Such agencies are liable to be seen as time-inconsistent: the government has an incentive to reassure the private sector, but may have an incentive to override the agency should the private sector be induced to make commitments. Private agents are liable to face the 'rotten descendant' problem. While they may interpret the government that establishes such agencies as a responsible government, they may doubt that a future populist government would regard the restraints as binding. They are also liable to face the signalling problem. The establishment of domestic agencies of restraint can equally be done by responsible governments and by governments that have no intention of being bound by them. This is the problem of poor reputation. A government that has repeatedly ignored the rule of law will have less of an investment in reputation than one with a history of abiding by the law and so has less of an incentive to obey a new restraint.

Specifically, consider whether it would be possible to have an independent national central bank in Africa. Cukierman, Webb and Negapti (1992) show that although in developed countries there is a relationship between the degree of legal independence of central banks and the rate of inflation, in developing countries historically there has been no such relationship. Legal independence has simply been overridden by the abuse of government power. Recently, however, two models of central bank independence have had some success outside Africa, the currency board model used by Argentina and the 'contract' model pioneered by New Zealand. We now consider whether these models might be applicable.

In the currency board model the central bank is required to back its liabilities with foreign currency assets as opposed to claims on the government. Yet the accumulation of assets this requires runs directly into both the 'rotten descendant' and the 'endogenous rotten descendent' problems. In the latter case the attempt at restraint actually induces the fiscal populism it is meant to avoid. For example, it could credibly be argued that the fiscal populism of Nkruma was induced by the very large reserves that had previously been built up by the cocoa stabilization fund.

The New Zealand model is particularly pertinent for Africa, since it is the only government with a British-style constitution that has created an independent central bank. This is an ingenious compromise with parliamentary sovereignty. The government, not the central bank, explicitly chooses the inflation rate; the governor of the central bank is then contractually obliged to achieve this rate, with a financial incentive for doing so. Whereas with a fully independent central bank the government is absolved of responsibility for inflation, the New Zealand arrangement by contrast forces the government to take explicit responsibility for it. The government is precluded from announcing a low inflation target while delivering high inflation policies: it gets the inflation it announces.

For the system to deliver low inflation, as it has done in New Zealand, four features are required that are not prevalent in Africa. First, the central bank must be able to deliver the government inflation target regardless of the fiscal choices made by the government. If the government chooses a low inflation target but runs a large fiscal deficit, the bank delivers the low inflation by forcing up interest rates. In Africa, with the exception of South Africa, domestic financial markets are too small, both absolutely and relative to the likely degree of fiscal indiscipline they would need to contain, for the central bank to be able to deliver on its contract. Second, there must be sufficient electoral dislike of inflation that it is political suicide for the government to choose other than a low inflation target. In Africa, although there is some electoral pressure for low inflation, announced inflation targets are not a significant feature of political discourse. Third, there must be trust in the official consumer price index as an objective measure of outcomes. Yet African governments have a history of using price controls, which create a gulf between measured and actual inflation, and are widely suspected (probably wrongly) of directly manipulating the official index. Fourth, the government must be trusted to honour its contract with the central bank governor. Yet some governments have such a poor record of honouring contracts that this would be doubted. Indeed, a recognition of the reality of personalized rather than constitutional authority possessed by central bank governors in Africa is that five governments have recently appointed non-Africans to the position. Though we shall argue that Africa needs to use external agencies of restraint, there are better ones than the resort to foreign governors of central banks.

Central banks are not the only type of domestic agency of restraint. Indeed, because of the dominance of fiscal policy over monetary policy in Africa, recent innovations in restraint have been directed more closely at fiscal policy. One example is the cash budget rule and another is the inclusion of long tax holidays in published investment codes. These attempts at institution-building are not futile, but by the revealed behaviour of investors, they have had only limited credibility. Until the rule of law has become well established, governments will lack the power to create domestic agencies of restraint with sufficient credibility to secure the private investment Africa needs. Hence, we now turn to the construction of external agencies.

4.4 EXTERNAL AGENCIES OF RESTRAINT FOR AFRICA: THE CONDITIONALITY EXPERIMENT

Faced with the African economic policy deterioration of 1970–90, donors attempted to meet the need for agencies of restraint by linking charity and threats. Donor conditions can be viewed as an attempt to create an external agency of restraint.

External agencies of restraint do not suffer from the problem faced by domestic agencies, namely the weakness of the rule of law. However, to be effective they must meet two conditions: (1) they must have penalties at their disposal sufficient to deter, plus an incentive to invoke these penalties; and (2) in order for the government to subject itself to an external agency, it must be confident that the interest of the agency is congruent with the interest of the government, so that the agency will not abuse its power to extract behaviour the government does not choose. Donor conditionality suffered from a failure to meet these conditions and so has proved ineffective.

That aid has been ineffective can be seen from three relationships:

(1) aid has reduced rather than enhanced growth (Boone, 1995);
(2) aid has reduced the inflow of private investment; and
(3) aid has been associated with a deterioration in macroeconomic policy; either aid has been targeted on those countries in which policies have been most deficient, or (more likely) it has reduced the pressure on governments to implement reforms (Collier, 1994).

Each of these three pieces of evidence is disturbing, but they also fit together. If aid is associated with policy deterioration, then it will indeed be associated with a decline in private commitment. If policy deteriorates and private commitment is reduced, then growth will suffer.

The budget-relaxing income effect of aid evidently outweighs any substitution effect of linking aid to policy change. This is probably because donor conditionality has failed to provide a credible threat. Although the ostensible rationale for policy-based lending was to meet the costs of adjustment, this was a fiction. The true rationale was that a quick disbursing funding mechanism was needed to stave off impending problems of meeting debt service payments. Lending tied to policy change provided a means of funding debt service even if there were implementation difficulties with projects. Given this agenda, the suspension of programme aid in the event of a failure to deliver on promised policy reforms was a threat of limited credibility, since suspension would trigger the debt service default the donors desired to avoid. Thus, the donors lacked the incentive to inflict punishment and successive waivers of conditions eroded such credibility as they had. In effect, the international agencies that policed the conditions were impaired by their preferred creditor status. Their self-imposed inability to write down any debts came to be interpreted as a need to maintain the ability of borrowers to service their debts by fresh lending.

The second weakness of donor conditionality is that, despite its ineffectiveness, it is deeply resented by governments. This is because the conditions attached to aid reflect not just those appropriate for an agency of restraint, but also those of a principal with its own agenda. The donors have preferences that differ from those of African governments and they attempt to impose these preferences, albeit fairly ineffectually. Conditionality is in part conceived as an attempt to bribe governments into adopting policies they otherwise would not choose. That this creates severe time consistency and signalling problems is well understood, a critique now familiar under the slogan of 'ownership'. However, the point here is that the attempt at bribery signals to the government that the donor has distinct preferences and aspires to impose them. A second feature of conditionality is paternalism; the attempt to specify the composition of the public expenditure financed by the counterpart funds generated by aid. Again, this signals to the government that the donor has different preferences and intends to impose those preferences. The use of conditionality for bribery and paternalism thus undermines such potential as it might otherwise have for use as an external agency of restraint. Recall that the essence of such a role is that the government should trust the agency to share its own preferences so that it will only use its power to restrain behaviour of which the government itself would (normally) disapprove.

In using donor conditionality for bribery and paternalism rather than restraint, the international agencies have, in fact, departed from their own traditional role. For example, right through the 1980s the record for the largest IMF loan ever made continued to be held by that to the British government in 1976. The government faced a credibility problem exemplified by a severe run on the pound that had precipitated the crisis. The government chose not to repay the loan during the next three years, despite being in a position to do so. This was because it wished to signal to the domestic and foreign private sector that fiscal and monetary policy would remain conservative and the most convincing way of giving this signal available to the government was that policy was bound by the undertakings to and inspections by the IMF. The British government of the late 1970s thus recognized that it faced a credibility problem that could not be solved only by the creation of domestic agencies of restraint and so used the IMF as an external agency. On the whole, the credibility problem facing the British government in 1976 was similar to, though less severe than, those now faced by many African governments. The British government that wished to behave prudently post-1976 was the same government that had ploughed into a fiscal crisis; thus, as with many African governments, it faced a more difficult problem than had it been a new government. The British government was able to use the IMF as an agency of restraint because neither of the factors that weaken donor conditionality in this role for African governments applied. The IMF did not have to continue lending to Britain in order to stave off default on its own debt, and it imposed no additional agenda beyond that which the government itself wished to adopt.

This example shows that in principle the international agencies can function as agencies of restraint. For them now to do so for African governments would, however, require both that the problem of financing debt service be detached from conditionality, and that programme aid be restructured so that it reflected not a negotiation between a donor seeking reforms and a reluctant government, but a set of commitments directly and exclusively chosen by the government. We consider these in turn.

For as long as the suspension of programme aid leads to debt default, it constitutes a nuclear deterrent: the penalties are too severe to be fully credible given the agencies that are implementing them. What is needed is to separate the financing of default-avoidance from financing that can be withheld with unpleasant but not catastrophic consequences. However, for this to occur requires the preferred international creditors to acknowledge that in many African countries a facility is needed for semi-automatic assistance with debt service, and this is tantamount to a debt write-down. A write-down would cause a down-rating of the debt of the World Bank, and hence higher borrowing costs for the higher-income developing countries. The supply of agency of restraint services should be seen as a traditional role for the international donor institutions that they have become impaired from fulfilling by their preferred creditor status. Since the maintenance of this status has value through the ability to supply loans at lower interest rates, there is thus a trade-off between these two traditional functions of the institutions. It is potentially possible to quantify this trade-off: the costs of higher interest rates versus the benefits of enhanced credibility. However, even without such an exercise it is evident that during the past decade the relative importance of the two functions has altered. The resource transfer role of the international agencies to the higher-income developing countries, except in the context of crisis, has largely been superseded by private financial institutions. By contrast, the proliferation of fragile attempts at policy reform, which private agents regard with suspicion, has radically enhanced the importance of the restraint role. Indeed, the periods of crisis that ostensibly provide the continuing rationale for the resource transfer role reflect this fragility.

Despite the new language of ownership, the practical conduct of programme lending has increasingly involved detailed intrusion by donor staff into aspects of public policy. This has arisen because the obvious and uncomplicated macroeconomic reforms such as the ending of foreign exchange rationing have largely been completed, and the reform agenda has shifted to much more intricate matters of the composition of public expenditure and the relationship between the government and parastatal enterprises. Precisely because such reforms are complex, the temptation is for donor staff to micromanage the reform process, so that the programme becomes conditioned on a myriad of administrative changes. Since neither of the parties to the negotiation can anticipate all the eventualities that will impede this progression, the programme carries a high risk that parts of it will not be honoured. The donor is then faced with the choice between waiving the conditions and thereby undermining credibility, and aborting lending because of some trivial breach. Further, such a progress of negotiation inherently places the donor in the role of pressing for more and faster reform and the government in the role of the reluctant reformer.

This combination of apparent reluctance and likely breach of undertakings does precisely the opposite for the reputation of an African government than what the external agency of restraint role is about. By voluntarily placing itself under freely chosen conditions, the government using an external agency of restraint signals that it is serious about wishing to implement reform. Virtually no government freely enters into a detailed timetable of policy changes, because in practical politics there are so many unforseeable events that there is a considerable risk of breach of promise and such breaches are very costly. Western governments choose the ground on which they make commitments quite sparingly. If the central task of restraint is viewed as the restoration of private investment, then it is evident that a detailed timetable of future reform would not be appropriate. First, investors are likely to heavily discount promises of future reform. If the government means to reform, it will do so rather than promise to do so. Second, the main concern of investors is not the prospect of further reform, but rather the prospect of policy collapse. Hence, the parsimonious use of promising to donors would confine promises to the elimination of highly negative outcomes.

Paradoxically, the use of promising for furtherance of the reform programme as currently done can actually discourage investment. The ostensible threat is the 'nuclear deterrent' of a gross aid cut-off that would push the country into the uncharted waters of default. The investor may realize that it is likely that the donor will relent when confronted with the prospect of actually implementing the threat due to some breach of the detailed timetable. However, since the prospect cannot be eliminated, the addition of a highly negative scenario to which no clear probability can be attached increases the range of uncertainty and so discourages investment.

To summarize, the attempt to turn the aid relationship into an agency of restraint has to date failed. This is partly because the credibility of the threat has been weakened by the debt problem, and partly because the donors have contaminated the agency of restraint role with the objectives of bribery and paternalism. The outcome has been the opposite of the uncertainty reduction achieved by restraint. A trail of broken promises by governments and sporadic implementation of threats by donors has created a wide range of catastrophic scenarios the probabilities of which cannot be quantified but are non-zero. While these features are not inherent to conditionality, as with African governments, so do donors face the difficulty that the credibility of any reform is undermined by history. Although it is worth making the attempt to turn the aid relationship into an effective agency of restraint, the liability of a poor reputation will prevent such a transformation in the coming decade, during which African governments newly embarked on reforms will be in most need of restraint mechanisms.

4.5 EXTERNAL AGENCIES OF RESTRAINT FOR AFRICA: RECIPROCAL THREATS

Unsurprisingly, the need now encountered by African governments for external agencies of restraint has previously been encountered by other governments. The demand for external restraint was met by the inter-governmental creation of agencies that work by means of reciprocal threats. In trade policy the major institutions have been the GATT/WTO, the EU and NAFTA. All supplied mechanisms by which a government could credibly lock in to liberalization, the enforcement being supplied by the certainty of punishment by the other partners to the agreement. In monetary and fiscal policy the major institutions have been the Bretton Woods fixed exchange rate agreement underpinned by conditional borrowing facilities from the IMF, the franc zone (Bretton Woods with the IMF role played by France), and the EMS (Bretton Woods with the IMF role played by the Bundesbank).

The common form of these institutions is that they are reciprocal: the governments choosing to be bound by them also participate in the design of the rules and in the supply of enforcement. This contrasts with donor conditionality where the governments that are restrained are the borrowers and the enforcement is supplied by the lenders. This reduces the risk that the agency will use its power to enforce preferences that differ markedly from those of the restrained government and so makes the agency better suited to a restraint role.

The collapse of Bretton Woods in 1971, the devaluation of the CFA franc in 1994, and the exit of Britain from the EMS in 1992 indicate both that there are limits on the powers of external agencies of restraint and that they can sometimes accentuate the economic mismanagement they seek to contain. However, the record is on the whole impressive. The GATT and the EU have been able to enforce massive trade liberalization among their members for long periods. NAFTA helped to maintain liberal trade policies in Mexico through a macroeconomic collapse that would more usually have triggered trade restrictions. Bretton Woods helped secure 20 years of fiscal order before being destabilized by the Vietnam War. The franc zone achieved over a decade of fiscal restraint for its members before its rules came to be circumvented. The EMS helped France to overcome the fiscal populism of the early 1980s.

The question is not whether reciprocal threat external agencies of restraint are universally beneficial, but rather whether some African governments need them now. Those governments that have implemented reforms but which have low levels of private investment prima facie have a credibility problem. Attempts to overcome this by appointing foreigners as governors of central banks, and by signing up to detailed conditionality concerning future reform with the donors, have evidently not proved up to the task. With the exception of the franc zone, African governments have not made much use of reciprocal threat agencies of restraint. Instead, they have depended upon non-reciprocated relationships. In trade policy they have relied upon the 'special and differential' approach of UNCTAD rather than the reciprocity of the GATT. In fiscal policy they have relied upon the 'charity with threats' approach of the donors, rather than the reciprocity of Bretton Woods or the EMS. It is time for African governments to harness the supra-national reciprocal threat institutions to their own needs.

5.6 THE AFRICAN EXPERIENCE WITH TRADE LIBERALIZATION AND REGIONAL INTEGRATION

In Africa regional integration has strong political appeal but has achieved very little. Economists have argued that this is not surprising. Many of the regional schemes were designed without regard for the incentives of the contracting parties (Fine and Yeo, 1994), in particular without compensation arrangements in cases where benefits were likely to be very unequally distributed. Countries therefore often see no reason to implement the treaty provisions or to abide by them. The East Africa Community offers a striking example of unsuccessful regional integration. It collapsed in 1977 in the most spectacular way imaginable, with Tanzania actually closing its border with Kenya.

There is a more fundamental criticism than the one pointing to incomplete implementation. Most students of regional integration in Africa agree that the hope that trade policy could be used to promote regional integration by reciprocal discrimination between members of a regional scheme is idle. The argument is simply that most African countries are too similar in endowments (unlike, for example, the members of NAFTA) for such collusive trade policy to lead to substantial trade creation. In this view regional integration is (with the exception of schemes involving South Africa) at best 'vacuous' (de Melo, Panagariya and Rodrik, 1993) and at worst trade diverting. Collier and Gunning (1995a) argue that whatever trade creation may be realized through trade reform can be attained through unilateral trade liberalizations; on Vinerian grounds alone there is no need for regional arrangements. The evidence from East Asia suggests that such unilateral liberalizations are likely to lead to regional integration as a by-product.

Though in Africa regional integration has probably indeed been pursued for the wrong reason, it can nevertheless perform a useful function. Unilateral trade reform has often failed because, as noted above, it is usually undertaken in circumstances where trade liberalization is time inconsistent. In structural adjustment programmes there have usually been no incentives for maintaining reform and no credible penalties for policy reversals. In the absence of a mechanism for locking in reform, reversal of trade liberalizations and other economic reforms has become a serious problem in Africa.

Hence reform requires a lock-in mechanism. The franc zone offers a model of how a small, self-governing group of African countries can achieve this by a combination of a supranational enforcement mechanism and an external guarantor. If such a group formed a free trade area, offering reciprocal free trade to the 'North', then it would probably achieve lock-in of reform; the threat of losing privileged access to the European market would prevent a reversal of trade liberalization. In this case the purpose of regional collective action is not to promote intra-regional trade, although that is a likely outcome, but to achieve sufficient mass to be able to negotiate with Europe and to create a supranational enforcement mechanism.

A necessary condition for lock-in is, obviously, that a member of the union loses something valuable by violating its rules, for example by reversing trade liberalization. However, what is at stake need not be valuable privileged market access, but could be aid. In this case European aid to Africa (which now sometimes contributes to policy reversals) would help in sustaining liberalization.

In recent years trade liberalization has come to be seen as a top priority for economic reform in Africa. Trade reform is urgent because the existing trade restrictions are not only very severe in many countries, but also highly volatile. Some commentators (Cadot and de Melo, 1994; Collier and Gunning, 1994) have argued that this reflects non-reciprocity. African governments, having succeeded in being exempted from the GATT reciprocity rule, were free both to build up high tariff barriers and to vary trade policy over time.

The severity of trade restrictions is illustrated by the case of Kenya, which, while often considered as having followed relatively liberal economic policies, had an implicit tariff rate in 1988 (after several liberalization episodes) on manufactures in excess of 100 per cent (Gunning, 1995). For many years Kenya made use of 'no objection certificates': imports were allowed in provided the local producer of import substitutes signed a statement of no objection to import competition. In less 'liberal' cases trade restrictions have been much more severe. In the case of Tanzania trade policy was an important contributing factor to the country's economic collapse in the early 1980s (Bevan, Bigsten, Collier and Gunning, 1987). Ndulu, Semboja and Mbelle (1997) show that by 1985 the exchange rate premium, a good measure of the severity of trade restrictions, had reached 477 per cent.

The volatility of trade policy is an implication of the widespread use in Africa of trade restrictions as macroeconomic instruments. Many governments, wishing to maintain fixed exchange rates and holding negligible foreign exchange reserves, have relied on changes in trade policy to accommodate external shocks. Under such a policy rule positive shocks lead to trade liberalization, negative shocks to a tightening of trade restrictions (Collier and Gunning, 1994, 1998). As a result of such endogenous trade policies investors have been faced with highly uncertain relative prices.

In analyses of Africa's disastrous economic performance trade policy has long been considered a prime suspect. Evidence of the harm done by trade policies is provided by Easterly and Levine (1997). They try to explain why Africa grew so much less rapidly than East Asia in the period 1965–90. Their conclusion is that to the extent that the difference in growth rates can be attributed to policies, trade restrictions are the most important source of the growth differential. Since in their growth equation there is a strong neighbourhood effect – growth in one country stimulating growth in other countries in the same region – their estimates imply that trade liberalization has a particularly strong effect. If undertaken simultaneously by a group of countries, it raised the growth rate over the 25-year period by 1.4 percentage points (Collier and Gunning, 1995a).

Long before such evidence became available, many African countries had already embarked on trade liberalization. In discussing these attempts commentators have stressed two points. First, when undertaken in the context of regional integration such liberalizations have not succeeded in increasing intra-regional trade flows substantially. Second, unilateral trade liberalizations have typically been undertaken as part of structural adjustment programmes and these donor supported liberalizations have often been reversed.

For the first point the *locus classicus* is an excellent article by

Foroutan (1993). Her study is currently being complemented both by econometric work (Elbadawi, 1997) and by a number of in-depth studies of various integration schemes, both undertaken as part of the research programme on Regional Integration and Trade Liberalization of the African Economic Research Consortium (AERC).

These studies demonstrate that regional integration in Africa has so far not been successful. Elbadawi (1997) reports on preliminary estimates of a gravity model and concludes bluntly that regional integration has been a failure. This is supported by the case studies. First, in many cases regional integration has simply not been seriously pursued. A common feature of many schemes is that many of the treaty provisions have never been implemented and the institutions set up under the treaties are barely functioning. In many cases serious implementation is not even feasible; there is considerable overlap in the membership of the schemes and many countries belong to schemes with mutually incompatible provisions.

One of the oldest schemes, the 16 member Economic Community of Western African States (ECOWAS), may serve as an example. ECOWAS came into being in 1977. According to the 1975 treaty, trade liberalization was to start in 1979 and be completed by 1989. In fact, trade liberalization did not even start until 1990, 15 years after the signing of the treaty (Jebuni, Ogunkola and Soludo, 1999) and so far none of the goals set out in the treaty have been reached. ECOWAS is dominated by one very large country, Nigeria, and fear of Nigerian hegemony has made the other members reluctant to import Nigerian goods (at least officially; there is a thriving parallel market). Conversely, Nigeria is suspicious of the franc zone membership of its fellow ECOWAS members. To make matters worse, Nigeria reversed seven years of liberalization in 1993, including the trade reforms it had initiated in 1986.

In the case of one of the relatively successful schemes, the Central African Customs and Economic Union (UDEAC), a common external tariff was one of the objectives. In fact, as documented by Decaluwé, Njinken, Bela and Cockburn (1999), the members adopted widely different rates. In one case all six member countries used different rates, ranging from 8 per cent to 49.5 per cent. Similarly, the *Communauté Economique de l'Afrique de l'Ouest* (CEAO) is supposed to have a common external tariff but this is not effective and the members frequently use non-tariff barriers against each other. The PTA, which aims at complete trade liberalization by the year 2000, has so far made little progress.

The lack of success of the regional integration attempts is most clearly illustrated by the experience of structural adjustment in Africa. Typically, far-reaching changes in economic policies, including trade policy, have been achieved under structural adjustment programmes, but without co-ordination or even consultation with fellow members of regional groupings.

Foroutan (1993, p. 239) concludes that 'thus far [there has not been] any meaningful trade integration in SSA'. Indeed, the share of intra-group exports in total exports is minimal in almost all schemes and often has stagnated or even fallen after the start of regional integration. Only the CEAO (of which all the members belong to the franc zone) reached a share of more than 10 per cent.[1] Foroutan's conclusion is supported by the AERC studies. The AERC study for ECOWAS concludes: 'It has been difficult to achieve any of the objectives of the Community' (Jebuni *et al.*, 1999, p. 64) and the study on SADC: 'to date little progress has been achieved' (Lyakurwa, 1999, p. 18).

Would the schemes have been more successful if regional integration had been more seriously pursued? A growing literature[2] gives a negative answer: for example, Foroutan, 1993; Foroutan and Pritchett, 1993; Gunning, 1995; Collier and Gunning, 1995a; Fine and Yeo, 1994; Elbadawi, 1995). Srinivasan (1993a, pp. 23–4), discussing regional trade in South Asia, stresses four conditions for successful preferential regional trade arrangements in the form of free trade areas (FTAs):

(1) pre-FTA tariffs should be high;
(2) there should be substantial intra-regional trade *prior* to the formation of the FTA;
(3) there should be complementarity in demand; and, finally,
(4) the participating countries should have substantially different factor endowments.

Only the first condition is satisfied in the African context. The second of Srinivasan's condition highlights a major difference between NAFTA, and the African schemes. The USA and Canada already accounted for over 80 per cent of Mexico's exports prior to NAFTA, while intra-regional trade was insignificant in all African cases.[3] The structure of both demand and production is remarkably similar across African countries so that neither the third nor the fourth condition is satisfied.

In these circumstances nothing can be gained from regional schemes:

> In terms of Viner's two-goods, three-countries world, the extreme case (in which negotiation would be irrelevant) would arise if two African countries would both import good 1 from the third country, the rest of the world, and export good 2 to it. Formation of a customs union would then not change trade patterns at all and the African countries would clearly not gain anything from the union. (Collier and Gunning, 1995a, p. 392)

In this sense African integration schemes might indeed, in the phrase of de Melo *et al.* (1993), be 'vacuous'. The similarity (in endowments and demand) of the participating countries would explain both the lack of intra-regional trade prior to the union and the lack of effect of the union itself.

Of course the Viner model does not allow for scale economies. These might, as is stressed in modern trade theory, lead to trade even between identical countries. However, this argument is not very forceful, first, because the market of a union will (unless it involves South Africa) still be quite small and, second, because scale economies can be realized just as well by unilateral liberalization.

A consensus has grown that in Africa regional schemes offer no extra benefits compared to unilateral liberalization as practiced in structural adjustment. Fine and Yeo (1994, p. 1), however, go further and argue that regional integration initiatives are actually detrimental:

> Indeed [the regional entities set up to achieve 'deeper integration'] suffering from conflicting mandates, overlapping memberships and inadequate support, could well obstruct rather than facilitate promising linkages that would otherwise emerge from trade liberalization undertaken unilaterally by many African countries.

The similarity of economic structures of most African countries is not the only reason regionalism could not succeed. Foroutan (1993) argues that non-discriminatory liberalization is a necessary prelude to regionally discriminatory liberalization. She explains the past failure of regionalism at least in part by the highly protectionist trade policies most African governments have adopted. Until these barriers are reduced, the transfers generated by regional reciprocity are too powerful to be politically sustainable. When governments wish to retain highly protected industries, then regional liberalization creates large transfers of industries and revenues. The attempt to mitigate these effects by compensation schemes is too complex to be workable.

While trade liberalization in the context of regional integration has usually had little substance, Africa has seen many drastic unilateral liberalizations. Two aspects of these liberalizations deserve to be emphasized. First, typically (but not invariably,[4] the reforms were undertaken as part of structural adjustment programmes, at the insistence of donors. The role of donors provides a major difference from many of the successful East African trade liberalizations, which typically had little or no donor involvement. Second, many of the African unilateral trade liberalizations were reversed after a short period, sometimes even before being fully implemented. Well known examples are Kenya, which within a decade embarked three times on far-reaching trade reform and each time reversed the liberalization,[5] and Zambia, which started seven different adjustment programmes, all involving trade liberalization and all ending in policy reversal. Côte d'Ivoire twice within a decade partially reversed trade liberalization measures. The Nigerian liberalization of 1986 was slowly eroded and then finally abandoned in 1993. Zimbabwe initiated far-reaching trade and exchange liberalization in 1991. So far this liberalization has been maintained, but the government stance is not fully credible; there is a large fiscal deficit that requires either massive exchange rate depreciation (which would be politically difficult) or a return to trade restrictions and foreign exchange rationing. There is a similar concern about the sustainability of the liberalization in Ghana (Tutu and Oduro, 1999).

There now is a literature arguing that these two stylized facts are linked, that is that liberalizations may be reversed because of donor involvement.

Notes

1. Only just: 10.5 per cent in 1990 (Foroutan, 1993, table 8.3).
2. While it is true that the official trade data exclude the substantial parallel market intra-regional flows (which are particularly important in West Africa), these flows are pathological in the sense that they are usually responses to differences in trade policy and other interventions

between countries and would therefore be eliminated by coordinated liberalization. Cf. Cadot and de Melo (1994, p. 9) and Collier and Gunning (1995a; b; c).

3. It should be noted that Mexico had unilaterally liberalized its trade policy before the NAFTA negotiations.
4. A notable exception is South Africa (see Hirsch and Jenkins, 1995; Hirsch *et al.*, 1999).
5. See Reinikka (1993), Mwega (1999).

References

Aizenman J. (1997) 'Investment in New Activities and the Welfare Cost of Uncertainty', *Journal of Development Economics*, vol. 52, pp. 259–77.

Bevan, D., A. Bigsten, P. Collier and J. W. Gunning (1987) *East African Lessons on Economic Liberalization*, Thames Essay no. 48, (London: Trade Policy Research Centre).

Bhagwati, J. (1993) 'Regionalism and Multilateralism: an Overview', in J. de Melo and A Panagariya (eds), *New Dimensions in Regional Integration* (Cambridge University Press for the Centre for Economic Policy Research).

Boone, P. (1995) 'Politics and the Effectiveness of Foreign Aid', mimeo, London School of Economics.

Cadot, O. and J. de Melo (1994) 'The Europe Agreements and EC-LDC Relations', CEPR discussion Paper no. 1001 (August).

Calvo, G. (1988) 'Costly Trade Liberalizations' IMF staff papers, **35**: 461–73.

Collier, P. (1991) 'Africa's External Economic Relations', *African Affairs*, **90** (360).

Collier, P. (1995) 'The Marginalisation of Africa in the World Economy', *International Labour Review*.

Collier, P. and J. W. Gunning (1992) 'Aid and Exchange Rate Adjustment in African Trade Liberalizations', *Economic Journal*, **102**: 925–39.

Collier, P. and J. W. Gunning (1994) 'Trade and Development: Protection, Shocks and Liberalization', in D. Greenaway and L. A. Winters (eds), *Surveys in International Trade* (Oxford: Blackwell) pp. 206–33.

Collier, P. and J. W. Gunning (1995a) 'Trade Policy and Regional Integration: Implications for the Relations between European and Africa', *The World Economy*, **18**: 387–410.

Collier, P. and J. W. Gunning (1995b) 'Trade Shocks: Theory and Experience', mimeo, Oxford: CSAE.

Collier, P. and J. W. Gunning (1998) *Trade Shocks in Developing Countries* (Oxford University Press).

Cukierman, A., S. B. Webb and B. Negapti (1992) 'Measuring the Independence of Central Banks and its Effect on Policy Outcomes', *World Bank Economic Review*, **6**: 353–98.

Dabee, R. and C. Milner (1995) 'Evaluating Trade Liberalization in Mauritius', paper presented at the Africa Economic Research Consortium workshop on Regional Integration and Trade Liberalization, Harare (18–20 March).

de Melo, J. and A. Panagariya (eds) (1993) *New Dimensions in Regional Integration* (Cambridge University Press for the Centre for Economic Policy Research).

de Melo, J., A. Panagariya and D. Rodrik (1993) 'The New Regionalism: a Country Perspective', in J. de Melo and A. Panagariya (eds) *New Dimensions in Regional Integration* (Cambridge University Press for the Centre for Economic Policy Research) pp. 159–93.

Decaluwé, B., D. Njinkeu, L. Bela and J. Cockburn (1999) 'A UDEAC Case-Study' in A. Oyejide, I. Elbadawi and S. Yeo (eds) *Regional Integration and Trade Liberalization in SubSaharan Africa. Vol. 3: Regional Case Studies* (London: Macmillan).

Easterly, W. and R. Levine (1997) 'Africa's Growth Tradegy'. *Quarterly Journal of Economics*, vol. 112, pp. 1203–50.

Elbadawi, I. A. (1995) 'The Impact of Regional Trade/Monetary Schemes on Intra-sub-Saharan Africa Trade', paper presented at the Africa Economic Research Consortium workshop on Regional Integration and Trade Liberalization, Nairobi (1–3 December).

Fine, J. and S. Yeo (1994) 'Regional Integration in Sub-Saharan Africa: Dead End or a Fresh Start?, mimeo (Nairobi: African Economic Research Consortium).

Foroutan, F. (1993) 'Regional Integration in Sub-Saharan Africa: Past Experience and Future Prospects', in J. de Melo and A. Pangariya (eds) *New Dimensions in Regional Integration* (Cambridge University Press for the Centre for Economic Policy Research) pp. 234–71.

Foroutan, F. and L. Pritchett (1993), 'Intra-sub-Saharan Trade: Is It Too Little?', *Journal of African Economies*, **2**: 74–105.

Gunning, J. W. (1995) 'Regional Integration and Strategies for Trade Policy in Sub-Saharan Africa', paper presented at the 11th World Congress of International Economic Association, Tunis (18–22 December).

Hirsch, A. M. Holden, C. Jenkins and M. Bleaney (1999) 'South Africa' in A. Oyejide, B. Ndulu and J. W. Gunning (eds) *Regional Integration and Trade Liberalization in SubSaharan Africa. Vol. 2: Country Case-Studies* (London: Macmillan).

Jebuni, C., E. O. Ogunkola and C. C. Soludo (1999) 'A Case-Study of the Economic Community of West Africa (ECOWAS)' in A. Oyejide, I. Elbadawi and S. Yeo (eds) *Regional Integration and Trade Liberalization in SubSaharan Africa. Vol. 3: Regional Case-Studies* (London: Macmillan).

Jebuni, C. D., E. O. Ogunkola and C. S. Soludo (1995) 'A Review of Regional Integration Experience in Sub-Saharan Africa: A Case-Study of the Economic Community of West African States (ECOWAS)', paper presented at the African Economic Research Consortium workshop on Regional Integration and Trade Liberalization, Harare (18–20 March).

Lyakurwa, W. (1999) 'A Regional Case-Study of the SADC' in A. Oyejide, I. Elbadawi and S. Yeo (eds) *Regional Integration and Trade Liberalization in SubSaharan Africa. Vol. 3: Regional Case Studies* (London: Macmillan).

Milner, C. and R. Dabee (1999) 'Mauritius' in Oyejide, A., B. Ndulu and J. W. Gunning (eds) *Regional Integration and Trade Liberalization in SubSaharan Africa. Vol. 2: Country Case-Studies* (London: Macmillan).

Mwega, F. (1999) 'Kenya' in Oyejide, A., B. Ndulu and J. W. Gunning (eds) *Regional Integration and Trade Liberalization in SubSaharan Africa. Vol. 2: Country Case-Studies* (London: Macmillan).
Ndulu, B., J. Semboja and A. V. Y. Mbelle (1999) 'Tanzania' in A. Oyejide, B. Ndulu and J. W. Gunning (eds) *Regional Integration and Trade Liberalization in SubSaharan Africa. Vol. 2: Country Case-Studies* (London: Macmillan).
Reinikka, R. S. (1993) 'Credibility, Speculation and the Speed of Trade Liberalization, with an Application to Kenya', unpublished D.Phil. thesis, University of Oxford.
Rodrik, D. (1989a) 'Promises, Promises: Credible Policy Reform via Signalling', *Economic Journal*.
Rodrik, D. (1989b) 'Credibility and Trade Reform: A policymaker's Guide', *The World Economy*, **12**: 1–16.
Schuknecht, L. (1994) 'Political Business Cycles an Expenditure Policies in Developing countries', IMF working paper 94/121.
Srinivasan, T. N. (1993a), 'Preferential Trading Agreements in South Asia: Theory, Empirics and Policy', mimeo.
Srinivasan, T. N. (1993b), 'Comment', in J. de Melo and A. Panagariya (eds) *New Dimensions in Regional Integration* (Cambridge University Press for the Centre for Economic Policy Research).
Tutu, K. and A. Oduro (1999) 'Ghana' in A. Oyejide, B. Ndulu and J. W. Gunning (eds) *Regional Integration and Trade Liberalization in SubSaharan Africa. Vol. 2: Country Case-Studies* (London: Macmillan).
World Bank, The (1994) 'Survey of Investor Attitudes to East Africa', mimeo (Washington DC: Africa Department World Bank).

5 Linking Africa with the World: a Survey of Options

G. K. Helleiner

5.1 INTRODUCTION

The headline in a recent edition of the *IMF Survey* reporting on the IMF managing director's annual address to the United Nations Economic and Social Council (ECOSOC), proclaimed: 'Closer integration in global economy vital for Africa' (IMF, 1995a). In a later speech, the same influential speaker stated:

> Globalization offers considerable opportunities to accelerate economic progress throughout the world. At the same time, experience suggests that countries that are unable to adjust enough to integrate themselves into the mainstream of the global economy risk marginalization. (Camdessus, 1995)

In immediate and practical terms, what can such warnings and exhortations mean? Does globalization offer the same potential opportunities to all countries in the world economy? Are the governments of all these countries merely confronted with a dichotomous question – yes or no – as they consider their integration with the global economy? Are there never any costs or trade-offs? Can such governments not pick and choose as to the appropriate dimensions and modalities for such integration? Is total globalization truly inevitable? What choices do the small and weak governments of subSaharan Africa really have as they face the new globalized economy? Camdessus himself poses the issue as follows: 'the challenge for African countries is to pursue a[n] . . . strategy that enhances the prospects of benefiting from globalization, while avoiding the risks' (Ibid.).[1] This chapter will survey some of the options that may be considered as Africa addresses the question of its appropriate links with the world.

Section 5.2 briefly considers what sort of world it is likely to be. What is the likely global context for African decision-making in respect of links with the world economy, and what is new about it? Section 5.3 considers the various possible agents for linking Africans with the world economy, some of the advantages and disadvantages of using them, and some issues relating to the framework within which they operate. Section 5.4, by far the largest section, addresses some of the critical policy choices before African governments. There follows a brief conclusion.

5.2 THE EMERGING GLOBALIZED ECONOMY

National economies are today much more closely linked to one another than they were when the major international economic institutions of the United Nations were founded in the mid-1940s. The success of the global economy in the 1950s and 1960s, engendered by revolutionary changes in transport and communications systems, liberalized trading and foreign exchange arrangements, and other such impulses, brought increased confidence in the efficacy of 'globalization' in the economic sphere. Trade shares of GDP rose steadily, interrupted only temporarily during the 1974–84 period of exceptional global macroeconomic turbulence (WTO, 1995). International capital flows at first took place primarily through the mediation of transnational corporations (TNCs), but in the 1970s burst forth in dramatic fashion in greatly expanded international financial markets. International production, under the auspices of these corporations, though still relatively small – about 7 per cent of world output in 1990 – and concentrated in the industrial sector (Lipsey, Blomström and Ramstetter, 1995), expanded even more rapidly than arm's-length international trade. Labour migrations, both legal and illegal, also grew.

The downside of all of this exuberant globalization seems to be increased instability within the global economy and greater vulnerability of individual nation-states to external shocks. This matters greatly to individual developing countries because volatility of macroeconomic performance is significantly (negatively) correlated with economic growth (Ramey and Ramey, 1995), and good luck matters as well as good policy (Easterly *et al.*, 1993).

Both global commodity markets and major financial markets have been extraordinarily unstable for the past 20 years or so. The new global economy remains crisis-prone and undergoverned. In the face of potentially severe global macroeconomic turbulence, there is still no overall macroeconomic manager. Moreover, the rules and institutions that govern and constrain economic behaviour in the social interest within nation-states are still largely absent at the international level. Nor are there more than the slightest beginnings of equity-oriented arrangements to ease the inequalities in income distribution that are maintained and even generated by the unfettered workings of the global market economy.

Recent trends in the direction of globalization are impressive. Any discussion of globalization needs to acknowledge, however, that the relevant ratios (trade to GDP, net capital flows as a proportion of GDP, and so on) are not so different now from their levels at the turn of the twentieth century. They are only now climbing back from the troughs to which they plunged in the 1930s and 1940s (Pritchett, 1995). The current globalization is therefore probably not as historically unique, particularly not in Africa, as is sometimes suggested. When one looks more closely, the increase in trade–output ratios in the post-Second World War period proves to have been mainly the result of developments in manufacturing (WTO, 1995, p. 19). In Africa, where manufacturing plays a relatively small role, there has not actually been much change in this ratio over the past two decades (although there was a modest rise in the export–GDP ratio from the mid 1980s onwards). Even this very recent increase in trade openness in some countries has not been so different from the situation in their (somewhat distant) colonial past. Similarly, their marginal position in the global investment community is not a new problem; and it is not now, nor was it ever, entirely their own 'fault'. Indeed it is not unreasonable to elucidate aspects of their current constraints and predicaments, and some of their future options, by drawing parallels with elements in the African colonial past.

For Africa, then, the globalization question is now whether (or how) to try to move into relatively uncharted, much more 'globalized' waters. Of course, some important features of the modern global economy – the product of its informatics and transport/communications revolutions, and an unprecedented pace of technical change – are entirely new. Moreover, the fact of political independence provides opportunities for choice that were not always present in that African past! At the same time, democratization in domestic political systems may place new (political) constraints on economic decision-making. It is a dangerous conceit of those who simultaneously press both economic reforms and democratization upon African countries to assume that the 'democratic will' is always, or even usually, supportive of the particular economic reforms, including external liberalization, that they espouse.

How Africans should think of their relationships with the global economy depends significantly on how they expect the global economy to function in the future. Will it be unstable, anarchic and inequitable? Or is it conceivable that international reforms will democratize the major international economic institutions, stabilize the world economy, provide 'safety nets' for countries hit by shocks, and offer the prospect of increased equity in global income distribution? In the immediate future, the latter prospects may appear remote; on the other hand, over the much longer run, such reforms may well be quite reasonable to expect. It follows that a discussion of this kind must be clear as to its time horizon.

So as not to be drawn too far into speculative visions of the future, this chapter will confine its horizon to the next 10 to 15 years. Well-functioning global economic governance arrangements and increased global equity lie well beyond that period. Within such a time frame, the prospect is unfortunately for only modest rates of global economic growth, limited progress in global economic governance, increased privatization of international exchange, stagnant aid flows (at best), periodic macroeconomic shocks and instabilities, and even the possibility of a major global/financial 'meltdown'. In short, African calculations as to appropriate relationships with the world economy must allow for only limited (almost certainly diminished) reliance on the benevolence of the rest of the world, and must assign an important role to risk aversion. One should not be surprised if African electorates and peoples, when they are heard, demonstrate fairly conservative welfare functions, resistant to taking on unnecessary risks of exogenous shocks and/or overly rapid or dramatic change.

5.3 AGENTS AND TERMS OF LINKAGE WITH THE WORLD ECONOMY

The people, firms and markets of Africa are linked to the global economy through a variety of intermediating agents. The links themselves take the form of flows of goods, people, capital, technology/

information and other services. Governments in Africa and in the rest of the world have intervened to set bounds upon what would otherwise be the free play of intermediating agents in markets (and other humanly created institutions including transnational corporations). Controls over imports and/or the use of foreign exchange, taxes on international transactions, and institutional 'confinements' in respect of particular types of transactions have been the principal instruments in such governmental armouries. The fewer and the less effective are these instruments within Africa, the more open are their economies said to be. The increasing liberalization and globalization of the rest of the world's economy implies fewer constraints on these links from outside Africa (although some important barriers remain, particularly in immigration and trade).

Private Agents

In textbook presentations of international economic links, there is typically a presumption that all (or at least the bulk of) the relevant transactions take place at arm's length in reasonably competitive markets. With such presumptions, the key actors within Africa would be seen as indigenous African people or private firms interacting in markets with people or firms in the rest of the world. The initiative for linking Africa with the world would rest significantly with the decisions of Africans. As is well known, however, the indigenous private sector in African countries is typically weak. Where the local private sector is stronger, it is usually dominated by ethnic minorities or resident foreigners.

A significant proportion of private international transactions between Africa and the rest of the world (and probably within Africa as well) therefore takes place within the hierarchical systems or networks of transnational corporations. Data on intra-firm or related-party trade are non-existent in Africa. It is probably safe to say, however, that transnational corporate linkages (at least) dominate the mining, tourism, manufacturing and financial services sectors. In some instances, African governments have attempted to drive wedges into private transnational corporate networks via nationalizations and compulsory state marketing arrangements, but these have gradually been weakened or withdrawn in recent years in connection with liberalization reforms. Expanded foreign direct investment by transnational corporations (and associated international production) thus constitutes an important possible avenue for the management of future African economic links with the world. Such TNC-mediated links would presumably be primarily driven from abroad. Flows of skilled people, technology, capital, goods and services can be effectively managed through transnational corporate systems, but very few of them are likely to be based within Africa. (South African bases for activities in the rest of Africa may be an important exception.) Clearly, African governmental attitudes to and incentives for such TNC activities will be critically important to their future. There has been extraordinarily little new foreign direct investment in subSaharan Africa in recent years (see Section 5.4 below). Such new TNC involvement as there has been has tended to focus on management contracts, licensing and the like, rather than investment.

As far as the private sector is concerned, economic links between Africans and the rest of the world can be led by indigenous African firms, ethnic minority (and resident foreigner) firms or foreign transnational corporations. If there are otherwise attractive investment prospects and a totally level playing field, over the time horizon adopted for this discussion, foreign TNCs can be expected to play the greatest role in mediating these private links in most production sectors because of their superior access to capital, technology, skills and markets. The terms on which different firms compete with one another will be determined primarily by African governments, which may choose to favour or disfavour particular types of firms or even specific individual firms (always, in principle, subject to their international treaty obligations and domestic laws). There are clear policy choices to be made. For example, Malaysia has disfavoured resident minorities; Korea and Japan have discouraged foreign TNCs; Mauritius has sought a level playing field. This issue is discussed further in Section 5.4.

Governmental Agents

International links may also be intermediated directly by governments, either African or foreign. African governments have, in the past, frequently established export-marketing boards and state trading agencies, and/or nationalized both directly productive and service activities that engage in international trade. The imposition and management of foreign exchange controls by African central banks also constitutes direct intermediation of this kind. Much of the institutional machinery of the government of any open economy is likely to be directed at controlling or influencing the volume, composition and terms of international transactions of various kinds – goods, services, capital flows, and so on. Such governmental efforts have ostensibly been intended to overcome market failures and to promote national development or other (social, political, special economic) interests. Like the indigenous private sector, African governments have typically been weak and unable to translate their aspirations into effective policy practice. This government failure has motivated much of the liberalization of recent years both in Africa and elsewhere.

Historically, of course, foreign governments have also played a major role in the mediation of African links with the rest of the world. Under colonial arrangements, hierarchical administrative systems controlled from the metropolitan centres were the basis of governance in economic as well as other affairs. The 'centre' or its trusted representatives made the critical decisions. Flows of ideas, people and capital, channelled within a discriminatory framework so as to favour the relevant metropole, buttressed these control arrangements.

In more recent times, after African political independence, aid donors and international financial institutions played a similar role. By this time, of course, there was freer competition among the sources of trade, capital, skill and ideas than in colonial times. With their deeper reserves of capital, skill and managerial capacity, foreign governments have sometimes been more effective 'managers' of economic activities within Africa than the African governments themselves (or so the donors have believed). The result has been projects and/or programmes effectively run by foreign governments, or those with whom they contract, pursuing the donors' objectives and carrying little, if any, indigenous governmental ownership. Effective linkages between Africa and the rest of the world can thus be achieved via foreign governmental mediation as well as foreign private (transnational) corporate mediation. Whether this is a realistic or desirable policy option is considered at greater length a little later.

The Framework for the Link

Special and Differential Treatment

In the 1960s and 1970s, the developing countries put a great deal of energy into efforts to achieve 'special and differential treatment' within international economic arrangements. While they achieved some notable rhetorical and 'paper' reforms, such as Part IV of the GATT and the generalized system of preferences for processed and manufactured products, the total eventual value of such arrangements to the developing countries was not great. In the 1980s and 1990s, the industrialized countries (notably the USA) launched an offensive on the 'free riders' in the international system, by which they generally meant the more advanced of the developing countries. To the extent that preferential arrangements continue to be discussed, recommended and implemented, therefore, they now usually relate more to the least developed or lowest income countries than to the entire developing country bloc. This has obvious implications for low-income Africa.

The current and prospective value of today's preferences on behalf of the lowest-income countries (both African and other) remains both absolutely and relatively (to their exports or GDP) quite small. Some have argued that those who benefit from preferential arrangements would gain more from true equality of treatment and the 'lock-in' effects of more reciprocal international agreements. Should African governments continue to press for special treatment in international finance, trade, and so on, on the philosophical grounds that unequals should not be treated equally? Or should they instead seek to join the international community as full and equal members as quickly as possible?

No one seems to begrudge the lowest-income countries their special terms within the IMF or the World Bank group (concessional interest rates and longer terms to maturity). Nor do many challenge their continuing need for external grants or technical assistance from bilateral donors, NGOs and the UN system. (There is some debate about the appropriate size and modalities of such flows but not about the existence of the need.) The only contentious question in respect of the desirability of preferential treatment therefore seems to relate to preferential *trading* arrangements.

Africa's gains from the generalized system of preferences or from the Lomé convention are small, and with the Uruguay Round they became even smaller. No one argues, however, that they are zero. It is true that they are subject to unilateral withdrawal, which leaves the recipients highly dependent upon the grantors but the same is true of preferential financial arrangements and foreign aid. Given these countries' weak strength in the international economic system, it seems unlikely that participation on a full and equal basis would generate significant gains to the lowest-income countries, beyond those they already at present enjoy. There seems little point in abandoning whatever special economic benefits the international system provides, however small, in pursuit of a dubious principle and the even more dubious prospect of resulting economic gains. The new WTO agreement formally authorizes the continuation of preferential treatment for low-income African countries in many spheres. (It should be obvious that preferential arrangements in favour of low-income countries should be offered in as multilateral a fashion as possible, to reduce the prospect of 'spheres of influence'. Unfortunately, there is little prospect of such reform; preferential arrangements continue to be determined unilaterally by their grantors.)

Intra-African Discrimination/Regional Integration

What about intra-African discriminatory import liberalization (and associated more general economic co-operation)? However Utopian it may still appear, it has to be said that the creation of larger political and economic units would assist the process of African development. This is typically less a matter of preferential trade arrangements, however, than an issue of the under-utilized potential for broad co-operation in all economic affairs (Ndegwa and Green, 1994, pp. 96–111).

Recorded trade among subSaharan African countries remains relatively very small. Intra-African (non-oil) trade is *not* less, however, than the predictions of gravity models that are based on country size (market size and area) and distance between countries, even without intra-African trade restrictions (Foroutan and Pritchett, 1993; Elbadawi, 1997). It would seem, then, that there can only be modest gains from trying directly to expand this trade; it is inherently of limited importance. On the other hand, there is some evidence that African countries improve their economic performance when their neighbours are doing well: there are growth 'spillovers' (Easterly and Levine, 1994).

'Distance' between African countries is larger in economic terms than in geographic ones. The general infrastructure of trade has been biased in favour of trade with the (non-African) rest of the world, because it has been led by agents of that rest of the world. Co-operative efforts to build such infrastructure afresh would certainly be helpful – communications, transport, credit systems, and so on. So would a prompt return to current account (currency) convertibility, which 14 African countries have now achieved (by accepting the IMF's Article VIII).[2] So also would the development of a common regime for foreign investments and technology flows. The prime need is for generalized economic co-operation for development, not necessarily – or primarily – for preferential trade regimes.

5.4 SOME BROAD POLICY OPTIONS FOR LINKS TO THE WORLD ECONOMY

Where controls, administrative complexities and misaligned exchange rates create socially costly interferences in international economic relationships between individual African countries and the rest of the world, there should be no hesitation in unilateral African liberalization. International co-operation to achieve it is unnecessary; indeed negotiations over its details may even slow it down and may conceivably lessen the domestic sense of ownership of the policy reforms. The continuing debate in Africa, as elsewhere, concerns the appropriate *nature* and *degree* of any such liberalization with respect to transactions with the rest of the world.

Should one simply liberalize all such international transactions – in both the current and the capital account – to the maximum possible degree? Should any remaining import duties be levied at a totally uniform rate? There exists a case for such an approach to trade and investment policy – what one might call the 'Washington approach' (although it is not fully practised in the USA). It rests on the presumption that, while there may be theoretically sound grounds for governmental interventions in market processes, and there may even be some governments that have intervened with a degree of success, African governments that have tried to do so, for whatever purpose, have typically made a mess of it and are likely to continue to do so whenever they try. While markets cannot necessarily be trusted to get allocations developmentally 'right', African governments, it is argued in this approach, will almost invariably get it 'wrong'.

Alternatively, one can conceive of an approach that consciously seeks to make as many transactions/links with the rest of the world as possible directly *functional* to medium-term to long-term development objectives, as perceived by the policy-makers (see, for instance, Lipumba, 1994; Lall, 1995.) This is likely to involve selective and differential incentives and disincentives, and a more activist state. On the East Asian model, it could involve close co-operation between indigenous private firms and the state as both interact in more co-ordinated fashion with external actors – in pursuit of the build-up of indigenous technological capacity and development-supportive institutions. In this 'Tokyo approach', fewer private international transactions are likely to be internalized within foreign transnational corporations, and external capital inflows are likely to be more carefully controlled. Indigenous economic actors will most frequently interact with external ones at arm's length on markets.

Trade and Related Policies

Comparative Advantage and Government Policies

SubSaharan Africa's (static) comparative advantage lies with primary production – agricultural and, in some cases, mineral (and petroleum) production; this will continue to be so for decades to come. This familiar proposition has recently been buttressed by Adrian Wood's empirical research on the roots of comparative advantage in a world of mobile capital and differential endowments of human skills and natural resources (Wood, 1994).

But what does this imply for Africa's longer-run development and its future role in the global economy? Activities dependent on unskilled labour can be a technological dead-end, unconducive to the productivity enhancement and indigenous learning on which ongoing development is now generally believed to depend. Analysts from Adam Smith to Grossman and Helpman (1991) have called attention to the risks attendant on specialization in activities with few dynamic possibilities. Import-substituting industrialization, which was so imperfectly implemented and has attracted so much opprobrium from mainstream economists, was motivated significantly by such theoretical (and practical) considerations. There is still an unfortunate vacuum in the theoretical and empirical literature concerning the appropriate government policy stance in circumstances where static comparative advantage clearly rests with primary activities, that may be weak in 'development' effects. Economists still know remarkably little about the potential dynamic properties of different economic activities, and of different degrees and forms of specialization.

It can sensibly be argued, however, that unless the purportedly dynamic productivity-increasing effects of alternative production patterns manifest themselves fairly quickly, the more immediate gains from 'proper' static allocation are likely to dominate. Future gains, after all, have to be discounted at some, rough, social rate of interest; beyond 15 years or so, future possible gains simply peter away. The social profitability of consciously directing resources away from sectors with comparative advantage toward those with dynamic potential obviously hinges on the static costs of misallocation for the sake of possible productivity gains, the size and timing of any such productivity gains, and the appropriate rate of discount, all surrounded by controversy.

Despite confident assertions by advocates of liberal trade, there is still no conclusive evidence that liberal trade regimes are associated with greater overall productivity increases (Pack, 1992; Helleiner, 1994). But neither is there much evidence one way or the other that supportive government policies have such effects, or that some economic activities are more 'nutritious' than others in this respect (in terms of learning effects, positive productivity spillovers, linkages, and so on). If such government policies can only be driven by hunches as to future productivity effects, it may well be safer simply to resist the imposition of static welfare costs that are known to be greater than zero (even if their measured size is often small).

It can also be argued that productivity increases are associated less (or not at all) with production patterns than with inputs, notably inputs that can only be acquired via importing and that continue to generate productivity gains as global technical change continues (World Bank, 1991, pp. 88, 98). If that is the case, the focus should be on the acquisition of necessary foreign exchange – through exports and capital inflow, perhaps particularly through foreign direct investment, which frequently can bring other key inputs along (without pocketing all the resulting rewards). Allocation is then fundamentally irrelevant to the most important determinants of long-term productivity increase, except insofar as it affects the capacity to import; for that, *any* form of export will do.

Leaving the precise nature of export specialization to the market, however, imparts a significant degree of randomness to the eventual export composition and overall product mix in countries with comparative advantage in primary activities. Scale economies in processing, transport and marketing – even if such scale effects are weak in production – would generate locational decisions on the part of investors, if they were left to make them alone, that concentrate investments and production in relatively few places rather than whenever the objective conditions would make them profitable (Krugman, 1989). Externalities may further encourage processes of concentration in the evolution of the 'geography' of international trade (Krugman, 1991). The literatures on the economics of infrastructure and on the locational decisions of transnational corporations (including analyses of the efficacy of investment incentives) are certainly relevant here. However, they have not been integrated very well with that on international trade.

Trade theory and policy have unduly dominated development discussion. In actual fact, trade typically *follows* developments in publicly provided infrastructure, other malleable endowments and prior private investment decisions. To the degree that private investments are influenced by governments at all, they are usually primarily the product of other (non-trade) kinds of policies. Chile's dramatic success with the (non-traditional) export of fruits, wine, forest products and fish in the late 1980s and 1990s was the product not merely of the newly favourable real exchange rate. As well, and more fundamentally, it was due to specific public investments of decades earlier in agricultural and forestry education, research and development, and infrastructure, without which the eventual private response could not have occurred (Meller, 1995). Roads built primarily for military purposes have similarly played an important role in agricultural development in Thailand. In the modern globalized economy, private international (direct) investment and international trade are largely, jointly determined in the evolution of 'international production': they are all part of the same process. They should be studied, as much as possible, in an integrated way. It follows that government policies affecting incentives should also be analysed in an integrated way – rather than through separate approaches to trade policy, industrial policy, agricultural policy, foreign direct investment policy, and so on.

SubSaharan Africa's best strategic course, for the present, will certainly be to build on its primary production base; in most cases, this means smallholder agriculture. Paradoxically, the greater is the growth in the agricultural sector, the better are the prospects for more-than-proportionate growth in manufacturing and relative growth in the size of the industrial sector. But this does not necessarily mean leaving everything to the market and having no industrial or agricultural policies. Progress in agriculture and agriculture-related industry, and in other activities meeting the demands of both domestic and export markets, can be assisted by conscious governmental encouragement.

Among the policies that matter most in this respect are different kinds of support (including creation or support of relevant institutions) for research and development, training/education, and infrastructure, as well as the more direct instruments of subsidies, tax concessions, preferential credit, procurement policies and the like. Totally level playing fields (and national treatment for foreign firms) may not always be appropriate in circumstances where local capacity-building is of such dominant importance.

Industrial (or sectoral) policy is a 'dirty' concept in current mainstream thinking. Yet it is surely peculiar to think that governments cannot, do not or should not influence private investment, production and employment decisions at all. The building of appropriate capabilities and institutions, where action is much more difficult to quantify, may be as critical to success as incentive structures – which seem to have proven insufficient in recent African experience (Lall, 1995; see also, for Latin America, Bekerman and Sirlin, 1995). In this area, as in others, Africans could usefully draw on others' related experiences, particularly in low-income (or recently low-income) Asia. The advantage of the African latecomer lies not only in the possibility of technological catch-up but also in the possibility of learning from others' experiences with alternative patterns, processes of change and policies.

African policy-makers will require more information and assistance in the development of their industrial, trade and investment policies – based on solid supportive research rather than presumptions and ideology. Such research and assistance is what they should be able to expect from the international community, rather than the policing of rules that may run contrary to African interests and aspirations.[3] Predictability and transparency are likely to help the weaker participants in the global economy. But total harmonization of their domestic policies with international standards over which they have have little influence and endless litigation as to their proper compliance with the rules are not likely to do so.

Trade Liberalization

Of all the trade and exchange rate policy reforms that might be contemplated, changes in the import regime are probably the most controversial and difficult. Rodrik (1992) has noted that the 'political cost–benefit ratio' of trade liberalization is typically very high: five dollars of income being reshuffled for every dollar of efficiency gain. In assessing the desirable and the possible in this realm it is important to take into account the fact that import tariffs, licences, prohibitions and controls are typically the product of multiple objectives. The need for government revenue is among the most obvious; in the short run the alternatives to customs duties are fairly limited. No less important is the fact that many of the import barriers are the product of balance of payments pressures rather than import substitution objectives. It can therefore be quite misleading to introduce the question of import regime reforms purely in terms of the cost of protectionism (as does, for instance, DeRosa, 1992). Where import barriers originated with fiscal or balance of payments difficulties they can only be assessed in the context of exchange rate and other macroeconomic policies that are primarily directed, or could be directed, at fiscal and external balance of payments objectives. (Once in place, interests in the continuation of such barriers may accumulate and strengthen, rendering it politically difficult to reduce them again.[4])

African countries have already gone some way towards liberalizing their own external trade regimes – removing controls and/or replacing them with tariffs and/or currency devaluation, simplifying customs duties and their administration, and so on (World Bank, 1994, pp. 62–76). These liberalizations have usually been undertaken in conjunction with increased external finance (although certainly not in a period of buoyant exports). Apart from the beneficial consequences of simplification they have typically increased the relative price of exportables *vis-à-vis* non-tradeables, and this has been critically important to development prospects as far as incentives relate to them at all. They have also frequently reduced the anti-export bias within the tradeables sector, and this too may have been helpful. Less evident is the social desirability of changes in the structure of incentives within the importables sector, which have received more attention from external analysts and policy advisors than they inherently warrant.

The removal of disincentives and regulatory requirements for exporters is generally unlikely to pose serious transitional problems relative to the welcome such moves will certainly receive among export producers. Where inefficient state marketing boards or previously monopsonistic co-operatives are forced to shed workers in the face of fresh competition, however, there may be some transitional costs and associated political difficulties. Political (and real economic) difficulties may also arise if the export trade appears to be taken over by private monopsonies or oligopsonies or, in some cases – politically even worse – by foreign or ethnic minority interests. While some see state export-marketing boards as prima-facie evidence of closed economies and illiberal trade policies (for example, World Bank, 1994, pp. 81–3; Sachs and Warner, 1995, p. 22), there are solid economic arguments for their use in some circumstances. These relate to the possibilities for improving the international terms of trade, better quality control, realization of scale economies, the overcoming of private market power, stabilization and other social objectives. Many of these arguments have been, and continue to be, plausible in African circumstances. Privatization may therefore not be the panacea that some suggest.

As noted above, the social efficacy of alterations in the import regime are often less clear. There is a great need for increased understanding of import regimes and the impacts, positive and negative, of different kinds of import liberalizations. There is far more theorizing about these matters than there is hard evidence. There have been few empirical analyses, for instance, of the extent of the 'pass-through' to domestic prices of import liberalization (or, for that matter, currency devaluation) in different industries.[5] The African pass-through discussions have been concerned exclusively with the prices of exports, particularly agricultural exports.

What actually happens when imports are thoroughly liberalized in African circumstances? Is it reasonable to assume that the pass-through is always uniform and complete, regardless of whether there is competing domestic production, foreign ownership of such production, domestic or international competitiveness, full or low capacity utilization, or other firm or industry characteristics? And what happens to the composition of imports following liberalizations of different types? Has there been predatory dumping, as some allege (for example, of Thai rice or secondhand clothing), in liberalized African markets?

Yeats' (1991) evidence of systematic differences in import prices between francophone and other African countries suggests that there are further import pricing phenomena requiring analysis and explanation; the small country assumption and the 'law of one price' may be rather too simplistic for African import realities. Dare one even suggest that part of the explanation for francophone Africa's *higher* import prices could have been its *lower* import barriers (with consequent reduced competition from local firms and reduced incentives to under-invoice imports)?!?

Heavier transitional costs are generally anticipated from reductions and liberalizations in import barriers rather than export barriers. The average effective protection (in the Krueger, 1978, rather than the Corden, 1974, sense) against imports, or even against manufactured imports, may not change much initially in an import liberalization that is preceded or accompanied, as it typically should be, by currency devaluation. Even a fully compensating devaluation, however, will leave significant changes in inter-industry incentives as the hills and valleys of the import barrier structure are smoothed en route to a simplified, more uniform system. And, of course, there may be further such industry-level effects if there continue to be further moves toward lower and more uniform import tariffs. Some previously more protected industries and firms will thus always lose from liberalization. Whether they respond by exiting or by raising productivity, there is bound to be some loss of employment and incomes.

Especially in low-income countries, where investment is low and response capacities are slower, one can expect that the losses will be felt more quickly and in greater concentration than the possible eventual gains from redeployment and increased efficiency in other (notably export) sectors. Hence there is a strong case, on both economic and political grounds, for encouraging and liberalizing exports first – as did Korea, among others – and leaving major import liberalizations for later, after exports have been set moving. These arguments are particularly strong when the government is simultaneously reducing its expenditures, privatizing its assets and otherwise rationalizing its activities – creating further short-term to medium-term labour market pressures.

Opening fully to external trade can also affect domestic income distribution. It is often confidently asserted that in subSaharan Africa, trade liberalization and the consequent expansion of trade will both reduce poverty and improve income distribution. This assertion is based on two underlying presumptions: that agriculture will benefit relative to urban sectors and that export activities, not least in agriculture, are more labour-intensive than import-substituting ones. But many forms of export production are not so evidently labour-intensive – for example mining, estate agriculture, and some manufacturing. Many non-tradeable activities, including some food production, are highly labour-intensive. Moreover, some very poor people are net consumers of tradeables, including urban groups that have newly been put out of their jobs. Moreover, the skill requirements of export production, and even their (particularly working) capital requirements, may be greater than many have assumed and greater than those of many alternative domestic activities. The distributional and poverty outcomes will depend significantly on the eventual nature of expanding exports. They also differ in the short run from their longer-run outcomes. The short-run effects are almost certainly worse.

In any case, the available evidence does not (yet?) clearly support the traditional optimistic assertions (Horton, Kanbur and Mazumdar, 1995). Governments would therefore be sensible to treat them with caution – and to prepare to deal with the frequently nastier consequences, for which there is some evidence, of increased trade openness.

Credibility Issues

Credibility and sustainability are in any case critically important. If key economic actors do not believe that the new incentive structures will be sustained, the effects of reforms can be worse than nothing. The credibility, basically the predictability, of African governments' own trade (and other) policies is fundamental to their effects. If private decision makers do not see the new incentive structures as likely to be sustained they will not respond in the expected development-oriented way. 'Incredible' import liberalization, for instance, will bring speculative over-importing and hoarding of durable importables. Sustainability (stability) of policies is therefore likely to be far more important than technocratic 'perfection' – not only in trade matters but in general. It is noteworthy in this connection that African governments except South Africa have not been willing to bind their tariffs in the GATT/WTO at anything like their current low levels.

To the extent that the current problems of Africa are attributable to the incredibility and instability of its governments and their policy regimes, there may therefore be a totally different role for external relationships. Some have seen a potentially major role for external agencies in the provision of much-needed credibility and predictability to African policy-making and African governments more generally. The IMF, the World Bank, and the donor community have already been playing that kind of role. It could be performed, some argue, in better ways and by different parties. Reciprocal agreements with more powerful foreign governments, with significant penalties for malfeasance or abrogation, might serve to 'lock in' (render irreversible) the relevant policies to a greater degree than government proclamations or even donor conditionality can do (Collier, 1991; Fine and Yeo, 1997). The purposes of such reciprocal international agreements would include the signalling of the commitment of African governments to their new policies and the provision of an 'agency of restraint' on their possible backsliding. The consequent increased credibility of governmental commitments could provide some of the required longer-term assurances to investors that macroeconomic stability and incentive structures will be sustained, contracts enforced, corruption contained, and so on. Such backstopping of African governments might also extend to guarantees in international financial markets.

To be successful according to Collier, such arrangements, must involve the participation of both African and developed countries (the EU is suggested), and must be reasonably compact in size; he is evidently much influenced by experience in the franc zone.[6] Such an approach is obviously inherently discriminatory against nonmembers.

The main question about such credibility-enhancing arrangements is whether their price may be inordinately high. Thus far their advocates have overemphasized their potential benefits. There must be more serious consideration of the possible costs; for example, adherence to 'harmonized' rules and standards that may be inappropriate for particular country circumstances or overly rigid or both; or the introduction of discriminatory arrangements in favour of 'members' at the expense of fully multilateral alternatives. Rodrik (1995, p. 111) has noted that while 'deep integration' may constitute a highly effective 'commitment technology', 'some may find the whole idea too reminiscent of colonialism for comfort'. For the present, assurance of macroeconomic stability is, in any case, more important to most investors than the trade policy regime. And credibility in the macroeconomic sphere is better achieved by debt relief and financial backstopping than by trade and investment treaties.

Private Investment

A primary objective of development policy in subSaharan Africa must be the raising of private domestic investment (and associated voluntary private savings) from the current dismally low levels. In 1994 total private investment was only 3 per cent and 5 per cent of GDP in Ghana and Uganda, respectively, and these are generally considered relatively good performers. Irreversible commitments to investments in productive assets depend on confidence in property rights and in overall political, legal and economic stability. In Africa, such confidence has recently not been strong. Confidence restoration feeds on itself. If foreign investors make commitments in Africa they will encourage domestic investors to do so as well, and conversely. Since foreign flows, mainly official ones, still account for such large proportions of investment in Africa (50 per cent in Ghana, slightly less in Uganda in 1994), their role in confidence-building remains very great. At present, investors in Africa probably respond more to the signals of the IMF, World Bank and bilateral donors than to any measures undertaken by African governments. This is pump-priming of a new and different sort.

The search for total predictability and totally steady investor confidence is a vain one. Even binding commitments via external treaties do not prevent 'busts' and flights of capital, both domestic and foreign, as the Mexican crisis of 1994–5 and its associated 'tequila effects' clearly demonstrated. Like Latin America for the past hundred and some years, Africa is likely to be a 'rollercoaster region' (*The Economists*'s phrase, 9 December 1995). Still, there must be determined efforts to increase macroeconomic stability and predictability. Foreign assistance needs to be significantly redirected to these (and other social) purposes.

Indigenous Human Capital and Indigenous Firms

It is worth constantly re-asking a key question: what would it take to bring large volumes of Africa's flight capital, both financial and human, permanently back to Africa to assist in the continent's long-term development? The potential returns from increasing utilization of existing African endowments of capital and skill are much greater in the short to medium run than those likely to arise from attempts to create new such capacity. As noted above, the mobilization of such resources depends critically on the restoration of confidence in macroeconomic balance and the management of the economy, and in social and political stability more generally. Public policy may be able to assist by conscious efforts to indicate to potential investors, managers, professionals and skilled workers that their contributions to African development are truly welcome and will be rewarded.

The provision of adequate rewards to overseas African initiative, skill and capital may seem to imply a wider range for internal African income distribution. It is important to recognize, however, that this increased spread of African incomes has already occurred through the migration of indigenous capital and skill to other countries. If such overseas capital is to be repatriated, it is likely to require higher returns than those currently available within Africa. On the other hand, overseas Africans are more likely to be willing to offer their inputs at lower prices than the world market rates demanded by total foreigners. Despite some risks, public policy must devote attention to the clear improvement of conditions and rewards for the mobilization of indigenous capital and skill, including that which is resident outside Africa.

Access to credit and other supports has frequently been biased against small and medium-scale indigenous Africans firms. At the same time, there are often severe impediments to expansion beyond the very small scale at which most African firms operate (Bagachwa and Stewart, 1992; Liedholm and Mead, 1987 and 1995). Even a truly level playing field would be an improvement, but conscious favouritism for such local firms – preferably time-limited and tied to productivity improvements – can also be justified. Many of these measures may run foul of the emerging rules of the WTO, both those already agreed in such areas as subsidies, intellectual property and investment measures, and those yet to emerge as pressures for 'deeper integration' continue.

An essential part of any strategy for drawing on the world's technology to improve Africa's economic future, whether through private or public channels, is the build-up of indigenous African technological capacity. Without the local capacity to understand, adapt, improve and in some instances transform imported technology to meet the specifics of local conditions, Africans cannot maximize the development potential it brings. Such technological mastery is obviously 'non-tradeable'; imports of personnel or institutions cannot substitute for it. It is therefore deeply distressing to see the deterioration of the universities and research institutions of Africa, and the increasing size of the African professional diaspora.

In the sphere of informatics – telecommunications and the 'information superhighway' – there may be unique opportunities for Africans to do some 'leapfrogging' through technological history (as Ndulu, 1995, among others, has suggested). The required hardware is not expensive and its costs are declining. What is required is the indigenous human capacity to take advantage of the new information technology's opportunities. This capacity may have attributes as potentially productive, and as essential for longer-term African development, as basic literacy and numeracy.

Foreign Direct Investment

SubSaharan Africa has not as yet been fully integrated into the newly globalized markets for capital. African borrowers, whether sovereign or private, have been considered poor credit risks by bankers and bond markets. The poor economic performance of most of Africa in the 1980s and 1990s – and its enormous and still rising debt 'overhang' – have, if anything, worsened external perceptions of creditworthiness. Foreign direct investors have also been chary of further involvement in Africa, except in particularly favourable circumstances with very high rates of return (Bennell, 1995; UNCTAD, 1995). More usually, SSA has been 'rationed out' of private credit and investment allocations.

Africa needs to attract private capital that is prepared to make a long-term investment in the development of productive facilities. In current circumstances this type of capital is unlikely to come to Africa unless it is permitted a significant degree of detailed control over its use. That is, any such capital flow is likely to take the form of foreign direct investment, and then only when there is a minimal degree of governmental involvement in what precisely it does.

Whatever one's view as to the eventual role of transnational corporations in African development, it is difficult to escape the conclusion that at least for the next 10 to 15 years, and probably much longer, they should be encouraged, along with other (domestic) private investors, to take greater interest in most forms of productive activity in Africa. For the present, most African countries desperately need their skills, capital, contacts and signalling role.

In terms of the likely size of direct investment flows, the best short-term prospects are unquestionably in the mining and petroleum sectors where Africa has long been, in the truest sense of the word, 'underdeveloped'. Exploration and development expenditures in mining were only an estimated 4 per cent of the world's total in the 1980s (IFC, 1995, p. 10), far less than Africa's likely share of exploitable mineral resources.

Tourism is another sector with underexploited export potential, in which foreign direct investment could also be confidently expected to expand. Greater developmental spillovers might be expected, however, from foreign direct investments in manufacturing and agro-allied activities, particularly where it collaborates with indigenous enterprises, including those of small and medium size – both in rehabilitating and restructuring existing dilapidated assets (often previously publicly-owned) and in new investments. Interesting innovations have been undertaken, for instance, in Kenya (and elsewhere) in contract farming (Glover and Kusterer, 1990). Unfortunately there is not at present much new investment of foreign capital in these spheres in subSaharan Africa. Foreign firms have been important players, however, in efforts to raise efficiency in these sectors and particularly in Africa's public sector enterprises. Management contracts (with private foreign companies) for the running of state-owned enterprises have been common in Africa. With some exceptions, these have been fairly successful – particularly when established and negotiated with the necessary care (World Bank, 1995, pp. 134–5, 149–50) – although typically not in increasing indigenous capacity. To the extent that privatization of state assets gains greater momentum, overcoming continuing political resistance and the enormous difficulties of doing it honestly and efficiently, foreign investors may also come to play an important role in one-off increases in government revenues.

Differences in the details of the modes of foreign direct investment and the choice of different instruments of private (or public) technology transfer to Africa can have a profound impact on the prospects for technological spillovers, indigenous capacity-building and longer-term productivity growth. It is now widely recognized that in terms of the purported longer-run objective of official technical assistance to Africa – 'achievement of greater self-reliance in the recipient countries by building institutions and strengthening local capacities in national economic management' (UNDP, 1993, p. 244) – the results have usually been poor. It would be naive to expect that foreign investors or commercially-driven foreign suppliers of inputs or technology are likely to do much better. Like aid donors and their employees, they too are driven primarily by motives other than those of long-term building of local capacities and strong local institutions. They too push inappropriate packages, overuse the (demonstrably ineffective) resident export counterpart model, are extremely reluctant to transfer or delegate real decision-making power to locals, and favour short-term payoffs over longer-term results. Nor is there yet much evidence to suggest that performance significantly improves when foreign investors form joint ventures with local investors, whether private or public. Exhortation to improve their behaviour is no more likely to influence profit-orientated private firms than to influence aid donors, and quite probably less.

There is a major dilemma here. Commercially-motivated foreign suppliers of capital and technology are unlikely to come to Africa unless they have a fairly free hand; yet that freedom to manoeuvre is unlikely to engender the kinds of change towards local capacity-building that Africans now more clearly seek. At the same time, the typical African state is too 'soft' and too fiscally constrained to be very effective about influencing these outcomes either.

Exhortation directed at aid donors, foreign investors and suppliers (and, in some cases, even African governments) cannot do any harm. Codes of conduct for foreign business and principles for effective aid might at least serve to remind the key players of what the social objectives are supposed to be, even if they are not always observed. More complete information on current practices and their effects may also help a little, and in any case is an intellectually challenging area for research. Real innovation in mechanisms to provide technology that will achieve real transfer, capacity-building and long-term productivity growth in Africa is needed. For this, it is probably best to rely on institutions that have these as their express objectives while working with highly specialized knowledge and within the context of the private sector. The IFC and the African Development Bank have special responsibilities and opportunities in this sphere. So does the Commonwealth Development Corporation. Some of the other bilateral donors have analogous institutions or programmes; those that do not might acquire them.

It is startling, and distressing, in this context to note the evident difficulty that the IFC has had with its much-ballyhooed Africa programmes (the African Project Development Facility and the African Management Services Company, launched in 1986, followed by the African Enterprise Facility, in 1989, and the Enterprise Support Service of Africa, in 1994). Except for investments in mining, mainly in Ghana, the IFC's investments in Africa have been of very small relative size – about $600 000 on average (against a 1994 IFC average elsewhere of $12.3 m.) – and have never grown at as rapid a rate as originally hoped. Its new investments in Africa actually declined in its otherwise expansionary investment phase in 1992–4. By 1994, subSaharan Africa's share of IFC's investments was about half the levels of the 1970s and 1980s. At this stage of Africa's progress, it seems that the bulk of such external support has to take the form of training, ground preparation and stage-setting rather than actual investment.[7]

Foreign Portfolio Capital

Direct investment, involving direct control over African enterprises, is the most likely form of foreign private capital flow to Africa in the immediate future. Nonetheless, there have recently been some promising beginnings of broader and more flexible approaches from portfolio investors. These have taken the form of new 'Africa funds' organized by institutional investors.

The fact that Africa remains for the present a relatively unattractive venue for the world's long-term investors does not free African governments from the need to develop suitable approaches to global financial markets or to consider the capital account effects of domestic fiscal and monetary policies. Orthodox policy recommendations have frequently been crude and undifferentiated: liberalize both the domestic financial market and the market for foreign exchange, including the capital account at the same time as restoring or maintaining macroeconomic balance. Where financial institutions are fragile (or even already basically insolvent) and prudential supervision weak, as in Africa, this may not be a sensible course. For countries of the subSaharan African type, financial opening may even be hazardous and harmful.

One would not expect investors, either within Africa or internationally, to be highly responsive to changes in African interest rates in normal circumstances. Other influences – inflationary and exchange rate expectations, the credibility of government policies, 'confidence', and the like – certainly dominate portfolio decisions in a context in which African borrowers are seen as broadly uncreditworthy to begin with. Marginal interest rate changes will certainly be of small import to global investors. But sharp macroeconomic restraint and financial liberalization can quickly produce *very* high real interest rates – rate changes that are far from marginal (with correspondingly dramatic effects for domestic balance sheets, especially in the financial sector, and for governmental debt service costs). To such interest rate changes – often coupled with a degree of increase in government credibility and investor confidence – some foreign investors *will* respond. Private capital may surge in – bringing what has been recently (and aptly) labelled 'Uganda disease', a phenomenon also found in Ghana, Kenya, Zambia and Zimbabwe, among others. In 1993–4, for example, private capital inflows to Uganda reached an extraordinary 8 per cent of GDP! (See Kasekende and Martin, 1995 and Kasekende, Kitabire and Martin, 1996.) The result is real appreciation of the currency, and associated problems both for short-term macroeconomic management and for longer-term development (particularly of exports and import substitutes). Private capital flows have been shown to be significantly related to the differential between African and global interest rates, just as they are in other places, at least over the ranges experienced in recent years (Asea and Reinhart, 1995).

Advice to open up the capital account, such as often flows from the IMF, needs to be carefully weighed against the counterarguments. International financial integration poses major risks for small countries with fragile domestic banking and financial systems. While on the one hand it may increase the efficiency of the financial services sector and diversify its overall portfolio and thus its risks (though perhaps via external ownership and control), it also increases vulnerability to the turbulence of foreign financial markets and constrains the potential for independent monetary and exchange rate policies. Further, there may be serious difficulties in the transition from a controlled system to an open capital account. Marrying a very thin, immature and therefore volatile set of domestic financial markets to the notoriously volatile (and huge) global financial and exchange rate system may be foolhardly.

There are thus powerful arguments for the use of capital controls, direct or indirect or both, over both inflows and outflows, as part of the armoury of African macroeconomic and/or development (notably fiscal) policy instruments. At a minimum, they can 'buy time', like reserves, for the deployment of other more fundamental policy instruments.

Of course, restrictions and controls – whether direct or indirect – also involve social (as well as private) costs. Notably, these are the cost of the administrative systems they require, microeconomic/allocative distortions, and increasing resort to illegal or informal financial transactions. It is well known that controls over the external capital account or cross-border payments taxes are difficult to police. It is also known that the new technologies in international financial markets have probably increased the difficulties. The efficacy of such controls or taxes also probably declined over time as market participants find new avenues for evasion. But it does not follow that they therefore cannot work at all and/or that they need to be eliminated and governments forever forsworn against their future use. When formal financial institutions are simple and few, there can be considerable macroeconomic policy mileage in the deployment of both direct controls and indirect measures such as, in the case of inflows, increased reserve requirements against foreign deposits or taxes on foreigners' interest earnings or even on all transactions in foreign exchange.[8] The efficacy of alternative instruments of control over (or other policy response to) unwelcome surges of capital, in or out, needs to be studied in the context of specific African situations. So do the consequences of total liberalization of capital controls and interactions with other domestic reforms, where these have been introduced. Again, there is much to be learned from the experiences of other countries, including, in this case, Chile, Colombia, Korea and Malaysia, among others. It is encouraging to see that the IMF is itself evidently moderating its previous positions in this sphere (IMF, 1995b and 1995c).

It ought to be possible for all to agree at least that policies must be tailored to the specifics of local conditions, as shown in a comparison of recent Ugandan and Zambian policy reforms. Exchange controls were previously so ineffective in Uganda that their complete liberalization probably had very little practical effect. Where, however, they were still to some degree binding on would-be capital exporters, as in Zambia in 1992–3, liberalization permitted significant substitution out of the local currency and thus losses in seigniorage for an already fiscally stressed Zambian government (Adam, 1995).

Official Development Assistance

Official development assistance is relatively more important in subSaharan Africa than in any other region. Africa's aid dependence has been lamented for two decades or more. Some might say that aid to Africa has consequently already been studied to death. Yet there has been little hard analysis of its likely future role as an instrument for the linking of African economies to the global economy.

Too much of the analysis of foreign assistance has been motivated by fairly crude donor (or international financial institution) concerns as to whether it is 'working', rather than a desire to understand how it influences particular economies when provided in different forms and in different circumstances. Much of this work has been highly aggregative, not bothering to make distinctions between project assistance, commodity assistance, technical cooperation and balance of payments or fiscal (programme) assistance. It has also often proven inconclusive and controversial, with different approaches to evaluation yielding strikingly different results.

For example, a recent IMF-sponsored analysis of the 1986–92 period (Hadjimichael *et al.*, 1995) indicates that the much-cited evidence to the effect that aid in Africa has zero or even negative effects is potentially quite misleading. The relationship between aid and growth, the authors find, is non-linear, positive up to a certain threshold – of about 25 per cent of GDP – and negative thereafter. Aid appears to raise per capita GDP growth significantly among countries with protracted macroeconomic balance. Among 'sustained adjusters' in Africa, foreign aid was associated with higher domestic savings and both private and government investment.[9]

The IMF, World Bank and aid donors used to project the foreign capital requirements for the achievement of national development objectives. The objectives of these exercises were soon altered; they became projections of aid flows that were likely to be available to individual countries. These were then used both to make reasonable projections of development prospects and to exhort aid donors to do slightly better. The concept of aid as a genuine 'gap filler' has long since vanished.

If further aggregative analysis is to be undertaken, the community of aid recipients could profit from a little more assessment of the aggregate net flows and transfers (and, even better, their quality) from individual donors and creditors. The international community at present seems to monitor every policy and performance twitch of aid recipients but keeps only imperfect track, on behalf of those recipients, of the changing behaviour of donors and creditors.

What is the appropriate future of ODA to Africa? What *should* it look like? How much should it be and what form should it take? What is its appropriate role in linking Africa to the world?

On the face of it, the aid relationship, as presently practiced, is a wholly unsatisfactory basis for linking Africa with the world. Too much or it comes in forms and on terms that undermine, rather than support, long-term African development. Aid donors and international financial institutions (IFIs) have been driving far too much of Africa's recent policy change, with the inevitable result that there is insufficient indigenous ownership of public programmes and consequent failure to realize 'societal learning . . . from societal mistakes' (Collier, 1991). It is unlikely that reforms that are pushed on dubious aid recipients will stick. While this is now recognized in aid rhetoric, the practices are driven by bureaucratic incentives and other interests, and are slow to alter. In the meantime, African governments remain too weak to withstand current external governmental and IFI pressures, and in many instances the aid relationship has probably made them even weaker.

Aid will have to be massively transformed if it is to serve as a major instrument for mediating Africa's future links to the world. Since such a transformation is unlikely and since aid flows to Africa are in any case declining, it is probably best to assume that the role of aid in African development will be *much* less in 10 to 15 years than it now is. (This is not to say that it cannot play some useful roles or that efforts to reform it should not continue.)

In actual fact, African governments now frequently have little idea of the total size or nature of aid donors' activities in their own countries. Significant proportions of aid expenditures go directly to foreign or local personnel or suppliers, without making contact with the recipient government's budgetary, accounting or planning procedures at all. In this sense they are similar to purely private capital inflows. No doubt many of these direct expenditures by foreign governments do some good, if only by raising some local incomes. But such aid does not strengthen the already weak capacities of African governments to develop their own expenditure priorities. On the contrary, it probably weakens them by generating an uncoordinated hodgepodge of public sector activities, bidding off some of the best and brightest employees from other public services, and reducing any local sense of ownership of development programmes. Worse still, these external flows are inherently unreliable. Such aid relationships do not therefore seem a very healthy basis for linking Africa with the world economy in the interests of long-term and sustained African development.

In the meantime, it is more sophisticated, careful and agenda-free analysis of the effects of different kinds of assistance in different countries (including debt relief) that African governmental and other aid recipients most require. Only with such analytical inputs will they be in a position to assess the implications of prospective changes in forms and levels of future aid, to press for appropriate donor reforms, and to manage transitions to new aid environments.

5.5 CONCLUSIONS

The new globalization of the world economy creates both opportunities and risks for the peoples, firms and countries of subSaharan Africa. Over the next 10 to 15 years African countries cannot realistically expect significant changes in the way that the global economy is governed so that their opportunities might increase or their risks decrease. They must therefore try to find their own new way on the basis of their own public policy approaches to a primarily market-driven world economy. Africans' options as to how to link themselves to the world economy are best considered in terms of a variety of different dimensions of such possible links. Simple, generalized solutions are unlikely to be optimal.

Among the issues to be considered are the appropriateness and feasibility of alternative agents for the mediation of Africa's links with the world and the overall policy framework – whether a level playing field or consciously discriminatory – within which they are to work. Indigenous capacity building is essential for the development of appropriate relationships with the world. In the medium term this may imply some favouring of local firms and people.

It is clear that for the present subSaharan Africa must build on the base of its primary production, in which it has and will continue to have (static) comparative advantage. This does not necessarily imply, however, a totally *laissez-faire* approach to trade or sectoral policies. Lessons can and should be learned from others' experiences with the benefits and costs of alternative policies for diversification and further development.

In the capital account, direct foreign investment has performed weakly – not least in developing indigenous capacity. It can nevertheless probably play an expanded and improved role in subSaharan African development. African flight capital, both human and financial, can also play a greater role. Confidence and, in particular, the political, legal, and macroeconomic stability that do so much to build it are critically important if private investors, local or foreign, are to commit firmly, to Africa.

Policy approaches to portfolio capital flows raise different issues. Complete international financial integration poses major potential risks and problems for African macroeconomic managers. Caution is therefore appropriate in this dimension of liberalization initiatives.

Official development assistance appears likely to decline. In any case, in its present forms much of it is of limited value to African development. Although major donor reforms are unlikely, greater African selectivity as to its makeup is possible and could be productive.

Africa need not succumb to mindless globalization via the state's abandonment of its role in the mediation of these links. Its policy-makers have important options as they consider Africa's future links to the world economy.

Notes

1. The quotation excludes only the common Washington linguistic 'tic' – the word 'adjustment', which adds nothing to the meaning of the sentence and may, in the current African context, sow needless confusion and/or controversy.
2. Three did so in December 1995 – Botswana, Guinea and Malawi; and Sierra Leone in January 1996.
3. The new intellectual property rules for instance, make no sense for low-income countries and in any case will be unworkable in them for some time to come.
4. For a good exposition of these interrelationships, see O'Connell, 1995.
5. There is some evidence that price-cost margins in developing countries (including one study in Côte d'Ivoire, Harrison, 1994) are related, though not statistically significantly so in Côte d'Ivoire, to the height of trade barriers.
6. Currency board systems seem to offer the prospect of greater stability but they also obviously involve cost. As Argentina's current difficulties attest, they cannot prevent unwanted *real* exchange rate appreciation and concomitant preverse effects for trade and capital flows.
7. Thank you to Jonan Haralz for this detailed information on the IFC.
8. 'A coherent case can be made for a Tobin tax in the context of stabilizing developing countries, which need to manage exchange rates and have relatively shallow financial markets, and where the cost of failed stabilization is extremely high' (Obstfeld, 1995, p. 188). See also Dornbusch, 1995; Williamson, 1991 and 1993.
9. Another striking result in this study is that government investment was five or six times as productive, on the margin, as private investment, though the latter may reflect the inclusion of some public enterprises (Hadjimichael *et al.*, 1995, p. 65).

References

Adam, C. (1995) 'Fiscal Adjustment, Financial Liberalization, and the Dynamics of Inflation: Some Evidence from Zambia', *World Development*, **23**(5): 735–50.

Asea, P. and C. Reinhart (1995) 'Real Interest Rate Differentials and the Real Exchange Rate: Evidence from Four African Countries', African Economic Research Consortium (May).
Bagachwa, M. S. D. and F. Stewart (1992) 'Rural Industries and Rural Linkages in Sub-Saharan Africa: A Survey' in F. Stewart, S. Lall and S. Wangwe (eds) *Alternative Development Strategies in Sub-Saharan Africa* (Macmillan).
Bekerman, M. and P. Sirlin (1995) 'Trade Policy and International Linkages: A Latin American Perspective', *CEPAL Review*, **55** (April).
Bennell, P. (1995) 'British Manufacturing Investment in Sub-Saharan Africa: Corporate Response During Structural Adjustment' (Sussex: IDS, Working Paper no. 13).
Camdessus, M. (1995) 'Africa and the IMF: The Challenges Ahead', address at the Society for International Development, Washington, DC, 14 December, mimeo.
Collier, P. (1991) 'Africa's External Relations: 1960–1990', *African Affairs* (July).
Corden, W. (1974) *Trade Policy and Economic Welfare* (Oxford: OUP).
DeRosa, D. A. (1992) 'Protection and Export Performance in Sub-Saharan Africa', *Weltwirtschaftliches Archiv*, **128** (1): 88–124.
Dornbusch, R. (1995) 'Cross-Border Payments Taxes and Alternative Capital Account Regimes', G-24 paper, forthcoming in *International Monetary and Financial Issues for the 1990s*, vol. VII (UNCTAD).
Easterly, W., M. Kremer, L. Pritchett and L. Summers (1993) 'Good Policy or Good Luck? Country Growth Performance and Temporary Shocks', *Journal of Monetary Economics*, **32**: 459–83.
Easterly, W. and R. Levine (1994) 'Africa's Growth Tragedy', Nairobi, AERC, mimeo.
Elbadawi, I. (1997) 'The Impact of Regional Trade and Monetary Schemes on Intra-subSaharan Africa Trade' in A. Oyejide, I. Elbadawi and P. Collier (eds.) *Regional Integration and Trade Liberalization in SubSaharan Africa. Vol. 1: Framework, Issues and Methodological Perspectives* (London: Macmillan).
Fine, J. and S. Yeo (1997) 'Regional Integration in SubSaharan Africa: Dead End or a Fresh Start?' in A. Oyejide, I. Elbadawi and P. Collier (eds) *Regional Integration and Trade Liberalization in SubSaharan Africa. Vol. 1: Framework, Issues and Methodological Perspectives* (London: Macmillan).
Foroutan, F. and L. Pritchett (1993) 'Intra-Sub-Saharan Trade: Is it Little?', *Journal of African Economies*, **2** (1).
Glover, D. and K. Kusterer (1990) *Small Farmers, Big Business, Contract Farming and Rural Development* (Macmillan).
Grossman, G. and E. Helpman (1991) *Innovation and Growth in the Global Economy* (Cambridge, Mass.: MIT Press).
Hadjimichael, M. T., D. Ghura, M. Mühleisen, R. Nord and E. M. Uçer (1995) 'Sub-Saharan Africa: Growth, Savings and Investment', *IMF Occasional Paper* no. 118 (Washington, DC).
Harrison, A. (1994) 'Productivity, Imperfect Competition and Trade Reform', *Journal of International Economics*.

Helleiner, G. K. (ed.) (1994) *Trade Policy and Industrialization in Turbulent Times* (Routledge).

Horton, S., R. Kanbur and D. Mazumdar (1995) 'Openness and Within-Country Inequality', paper presented to the International Economic Association World Congress, Tunis, mimeo.

IFC (International Finance Corporation) (1995) *IFC Review* (Fall).

IMF (International Monetary Fund) (1995a) *IMF Survey*, 17 July (Washington, DC).

IMF (International Monetary Fund) (1995b) *International Capital Markets, Developments, Prospects, and Policy Issues* (Washington, DC).

IMF (International Monetary Fund) (1995c) 'Capital Account Convertibility, Review of Experience and Implications for IMF Policies', Occasional Paper 131 (Washington, DC).

Kasekende, L. and M. Martin (1995) 'Macroeconomic Policy Research Issues: The Sequencing, Consistency and Credibility of Structural Adjustment in Africa', AERC Senior Policy Seminar, African Economic Research Consortium, Nairobi (March).

Kasekende, L., D. Kitabire and M. Martin (1996) 'Capital Flows and Macroeconomic Policy in Sub-Saharan Africa', paper for the Group of Twenty-Four, Washington and Geneva, mimeo.

Krueger, A. O. (1978) *Foreign Trade Regimes and Economic Development: Liberalization Attempts and Consequences* (New York: NBER).

Krugman, P., (1989) 'New Trade Theory and the Less Developed Countries', in G. Calvo, R. Findlay, P. Kouri and J. De Macedo (eds), *Debt, Stabilization and Development, Essays in Memory of Carlos Diaz-Alejandro* (Blackwell and WIDER, 1989) pp. 347–65.

Krugman, P. (1991) *Geography and Trade* (Cambridge, Mass.: MIT Press).

Lall, S. (1995) 'Structural Adjustment and African Industry', *World Development*, **23** (12).

Liedholm, C. and D. Mead (1987) 'Small-Scale Industries: Empirical Evidence and Policy Implications', MSU International Development Paper, 9 (East Lansing: Michigan State University, Department of Agricultural Economics).

Liedholm, C. and D. Mead (1995) 'The Dynamic Role of Micro and Small Enterprises in the Development Process', GEMINI Project, Michigan State University, mimeo (September).

Lipsey, R. E., M. Blomström and E. Ramstetter (1995) 'Internationalized Production in World Output', National Bureau of Economic Research Working Paper Series, no. 5385 (Cambridge, Mass.)

Lipumba, N. (1994) *Africa Beyond Adjustment*, Overseas Development Council, Policy Essay 15 (Washington, DC).

Meller, P. (1995) 'Chilean Export Growth, 1970–90: An Assessment', in G. K. Helleiner (ed.), *Manufacturing for Export in the Developing World: Problems and Possibilities* (Routledge) pp. 21–53.

Ndegwa, P. and R. H. Green (1994) *Africa to 2000 and Beyond, Imperative Political and Economic Agenda* (Nairobi: East African Educational Publishers).

Ndulu, B. (1995) 'African Development Challenges in a Changing World Economy', mimeo, Nairobi, 27 October (presented at University of Copenhagen, November).

Obstfeld, M. (1995) 'International Currency Experience: New Lessons and Lessons Relearned', *Brookings Papers on Economic Activity*, no. 1 (Washington, DC).
O'Connell, S. (1995) 'Macroeconomic Harmonisation, Trade Reform, and Regional Trade in Sub-Saharan Africa', AERC, Nairobi, mimeo.
Pack, H. (1992) 'Learning and Productivity Change in Developing Countries', in G. K. Helleiner (ed.), *Trade Policy, Industrialization and Development: New Perspectives* (Oxford: Clarendon Press for WIDER) pp. 21–45.
Pritchett, L. (1995) 'Capital Flows: Five Stylized Facts for the 1990s', World Bank, mimeo.
Ramey, G. and V. Ramey (1995) 'Cross-Country Evidence on the Link Between Volatility and Growth', *American Economic Review*, **85** (5).
Rodrik, D. (1992) 'The Rush to Free Trade in the Developing World: Why So Late? Why Now? Will It Last?' National Bureau of Economic Research Working Paper Series, no. 3947 (January).
Rodrik, D. (1995) 'Comments', in A. O. Krueger, *Trade Policies and Developing Nations* (Washington, DC: Brookings Institution).
Sachs, J. and A. Warner (1995) 'Economic Reform and the Process of Global Integration', *Brookings Papers on Economic Activity, 25th Anniversary Issue*, I.
UNCTAD (1995) *Foreign Investment in Africa*.
UNDP (1993) *Rethinking Technical Cooperation: Reforms for Capacity-Building in Africa* (New York).
Williamson, J. (1991) 'On Liberalizing the Capital Account', in R. O'Brien (ed.), *Finance and the International Economy*, no. 5 (London: Amex Bank).
Williamson, J. (1993) 'A Cost-Benefit Analysis of Capital Account Liberalization', in H. Reisen and B. Fischer (eds), *Financial Opening* (Paris: OECD).
Wood, A. (1994) 'Skill, Land and Trade: A Simple Analytical Framework', (Sussex: IDS Working Paper no. 1) (February).
World Bank (1991) *World Development Report* (Washington, DC).
World Bank (1994) *Adjustment in Africa: Reforms, Results, and the Road Ahead* (Oxford University Press).
World Bank (1995) *Bureaucrats in Business: The Economics and Politics of Government Ownership* (Washington DC).
WTO (World Trade Organization) (1995) *International Trade, Trends and Statistics* (Geneva).
Yeats, A. J. (1991) 'Do African Countries Pay More for Import? Yes', in A. Chhibber and S. Fischer (eds), *Economic Reform in Sub-Saharan Africa*, pp. 189–210 (Washington, DC: The World Bank).

6 Options for Future Trade Liberalization in SubSaharan African

Ademola Oyejide

6.1 INTRODUCTION

Regardless of their specific trade policy stance, the economies of most subSaharan African (SSA) countries have traditionally been heavily influenced by developments in the world market. The various trade policy initiatives these countries have taken over time, partly in reaction to their international exposure, have generated much debate. In fact, the World Bank (1981) attributed much of the fault for their poor performance, especially during the 1970s, to misguided trade policies.

Thus, in SSA countries 'trade policy recommendations are prominent in normative analyses of current development problems' (Helleiner, 1995, p. 1). Moreover, trade policy reform carries great weight in many of the reform packages proposed to (and increasingly implemented by) African governments' (Rodrik, 1988, p. 2). On the one hand, the relatively heavy focus on trade policy reform in the typical structural adjustment programme may, to some extent, overestimate the role of trade policy in the development process. On the other hand, the largely unquestioned identification of trade liberalization with import liberalization risks underplaying the contribution of trade policy to long-term development.

This chapter seeks to provide a more balanced picture of trade liberalization by focusing on both its import and export dimensions, and by stressing that sequencing may be necessary between those two elements of trade liberalization and within each one (Section 6.2). Proceeding from this, in Section 6.3 the chapter reviews the trade liberalization experience of SSA countries against the framework just established. It concludes, in Section 6.4, by offering a brief sketch of the context of future trade policy reform as well as the appropriate direction, content and sequencing of future trade liberalization in subSaharan African.

6.2 CONCEPTUALIZING TRADE LIBERALIZATION

When trade liberalization occurs by deliberate design, it does so through the implementation of specific trade policy. But trade policy is often confused with other, and in some cases more general, macroeconomic policies. It is therefore necessary to clarify what trade policy is and what its major components and instruments are. This section begins by articulating a definition of trade policy, and proceeds with the analysis of its major elements.

In the context of subSaharan Africa, trade policy changes constitute only one set of the many policy reforms being undertaken, usually under the general umbrella of structural adjustment programmes. However, this set appears to carry substantial weight in the typical reform package. The rather sharp focus on this component may be part of the reason why trade policy is often not sufficiently differentiated, or separable, from broader macroeconomic policies. Yet, analytical convenience and the need to relate particular policies to their consequences require that trade policy and its major components be separately identified from other policies.

Trade Policy: Meaning and Orientation

In general, trade policy measures are targeted at the tradeable goods and services sector. More specifically, they influence the overall structure of incentives within this sector and thus affect the relative prices between importables and exportables. In the process, trade policy measures exert their impact through changes in the incentives for producing and consuming, as well as exporting and importing, various types of tradeable goods and services (Helleiner, 1992, 1995). It should be obvious that while trade policy measures aim primarily at influencing the composition and levels of imports and exports, this does not preclude other factors and policies from affecting the levels of exports and imports. Clearly, exogenous changes in levels of income and/or general economic activity in a country would tend to influence both tradeable and non-tradeable sectors. At the same time, some macroeconomic policies (for example, exchange rate policy) could alter relative prices between non-tradeable and tradeable goods and hence influence the levels of exports and imports. Disentangling the effects of pure trade policy on the composition and levels of imports and exports from the effects of other policies and exogenous factors is one of the many challenges facing empirical research in this area.

Discussions of trade policy reform, especially in the context of subSaharan Africa, are confined almost exclusively to a debate about the pros and cons of trade liberalization. How far and how fast should it proceed? What should be its coverage? What measures should be applied and in what sequence? This contextual framework reflects the reality that many developing countries have embraced and are implementing various forms of trade liberalization measures. In many cases, the observed changes have been induced by policy advice from several multilateral development institutions (for example, the World Bank and the International Monetary Fund). Or, trade policy may be in accordance with the terms of financial facilities obtained from such bodies and conditioned upon the prior or concurrent establishment of more open trade regimes. As well, in a limited number of cases, the belief of the governments concerned in the benefits of trade liberalization plays a part.

Thus, in the context of this perspective, trade policy reform is coterminous with trade liberalization, which in turn refers to policy changes and associated measures that are used to endow the trade regime with a more neutral incentive structure. In the process, the policies aim to reduce domestic policy distortions and open the economy to the world market. A neutral trade regime is one whose incentive structure does not discriminate between exportables and importables or between production for the domestic market and for export sales. More specifically and, in the words of Helleiner (1995, p. 30):

> When the incentives for exporting are the same as those for import-competing activity, the trade policy is 'neutral' in its encouragement to these two kinds of activity. When such neutrality exists or when exporting is favoured in the economy . . ., the trade policy is generally said to be 'outward-oriented'. Otherwise, trade policy is said to reflect anti-export bias and therefore to be 'inward-oriented'.

The definition and classification of trade policy orientation implied by the above could be sharpened somewhat by eliminating the ambiguity inherent in the interpretation of trade policy neutrality as outward orientation. A three-part classification – that is, outward, neutral and inward – would clearly be more useful. This would require that trade policy neutrality be distinguished from an outward-orientated trade policy stance, with the latter concept being used to refer to a trade policy regime that discriminates in favour of exports. Similarly, an inward-orientated trade policy regime would be one that discriminates in favour of import-competing activities. Under this three-part categorization, trade liberalization would imply transforming the trade regime from an 'inward-orientated' stance that discriminates in favour of (and thus protects) import-competing activities into a 'neutral' regime whose incentive structure does not distinguish between exportables and importables – or even into an 'outward-orientated' trade policy regime that discriminates in favour of (and thus actively promotes) exports.

It has been argued that trade liberalization that produces either a neutral or an outward-orientated trade regime confers certain productivity-enhancing and growth-promoting features on the liberalized economy (World Bank, 1991). Included among these are improvement in the efficiency with which resources are allocated, increases in competition and product specialization, enhanced ability to attract foreign investment, and the creation of a favourable environment for technology transfer. In the context of a more open trade regime, technology can be transferred through at least three distinct sources: (1) as an integral part of foreign investment; (2) through increased trade that allows a country to import capital goods that embody current technology; and (3) through export competition that induces firms to operate at the frontiers of technology development. This perspective thus suggests, first, that a trade regime that enhances import and export competition would induce increased trade and promote more rapid economic growth; and second, that the key to the productivity increases associated with expanded trade lies predominantly in 'exporting [which] strengthens the incentive to adopt new technology by increasing the returns from innovation through expanded market opportunities' (World Bank, 1991, p. 89).

There exists, however, an alternative perspective that associates the growth-promoting effect of expanding trade with the productivity-enhancing characteristics of technology embodied in, and the increased capacity utilization permitted by, increased imports of capital and intermediate inputs (Helleiner, 1995). This perspective recognizes three main areas of gain linked to trade expansion. The first gain derives from the once-and-for-all gain associated with the re-allocation of production and consumption generated by trade expansion. A second (also once-and-for-all) gain emanates from increased capacity utilization made possible by the availability of 'critically important imports' upon which domestic production in the developing countries is heavily dependent. The third, more dynamic and enduring gain, from trade is technology-based productivity increases. Helleiner (1995, p. 15) argues that:

> It seems more plausible, however, to associate the main externalities associated with trade with imports, particularly those of capital goods and intermediate inputs (when they embody new technology) and technological and other non-factor services, rather than exports. Such imports bring the knowledge upon which long-term growth itself is now seen to be heavily dependent.

This perspective would, in effect, be consistent with a trade regime whose incentive structure discriminates in favour of technology-embodying imports of capital goods and intermediate inputs as a means of capturing the growth-promoting gains derivable from increased capacity utilization and the productivity-enhancing gains emanating from technology transfer. Even in the context of this perspective, however, there is a clear recognition of the important role of exports, not necessarily as the critical vehicle for technology transfer but more significantly as the primary source for financing the indispensable bottleneck-breaking and technology-bearing imports, especially in the absence of adequate capital inflows. Both perspectives suggest that the two (import and export) components of trade policy reform may have important, distinct and different implications. Hence, their differences deserve to be explicitly taken into account in the design and implementation of trade liberalization programmes.

Import Liberalization

The import component of trade liberalization is of special significance in subSaharan Africa for a variety of reasons. The standard instruments of trade policy, such as import tariffs and quantitative import restrictions, are often used to serve multiple objectives in this region, given the country characteristics that limit the availability and effectiveness of alternative policy handles. Hence, trade policy reform, especially as it relates to the import component, needs to be carefully designed to ensure that its full implications for the various objectives are explicitly recognized and taken into account.

The fiscal impact of changes in the form and level of import protection constitutes one of these areas of concern. Compared to other regions of the world, sources of government revenues are much narrower in subSaharan Africa. This narrow base translates into an unusually heavy reliance on trade taxes. In 1989, according to the World Bank (1992), six out of 36 countries in this region derived more than half of their total government revenues from trade taxes. Nineteen of the countries had trade taxes accounting for 25–50 per cent of their total revenues. In addition, import-related revenues provided over 70 per cent of total trade taxes.

Receipts from import tariffs represent a major source of government revenues that cannot be easily dispensed with. This is so not only because of their magnitude (relative to other sources of revenue), but also because mobilizing fiscal resources through other means and in comparable magnitude is costly, if not impossible, especially in the short to medium term. As Lyakurwa (1993, p. 36) observes, 'two revenue-related costs of trade liberalization, which tend to reduce the budget balance, appear to be unavoidable, even under the most prudent of policy regimes'. First, even though trade volumes could increase after liberalization, revenue from trade taxes may fall. As export taxes are virtually eliminated and imports are less heavily taxed, liberalization implies a shift from traded goods in the tax base to traded goods outside the tax base. Second, trade liberalization implies shifting from easy-to-collect trade taxes to more difficult-to-collect revenues from income and domestic consumption. These tax handles typically require more sophisticated accounting and record-keeping systems than are usually available, and tax revenue losses may be inevitable as some of the income and activities associated with trade liberalization escape the tax net. It should be noted, of course, that to the extent that import liberalization reduces illegal activities, including smuggling, it could expand the tax base and thereby increase total tax revenues derived from lower rates of trade taxes.

Import liberalization may lead to increased trade deficits and thus worsen the usually precarious balance-of-payment position of the typical SSA country. A deep, generalized and sudden import-liberalization programme could induce an abnormally high demand for imports, which could place unsustainable pressure on the country's balance of payments requiring access to substantial aid and capital inflow or a compensating exchange rate policy change. As Collier and Gunning (1992) demonstrate, although import liberalization does not inevitably worsen the balance of payments, it seems likely to do so, particularly in the short to medium term. Increasing trade deficits arising from import liberalization should worry the typical SSA country, which lacks flexible access to external financing.

To the extent that import liberalization gives rise to fiscal deficits and balance-of-payments problems, it would worsen the macroeconomic imbalance facing many SSA countries and thereby make the process of steady adjustment and recovery of growth more difficult to sustain.

In addition to their use for generating fiscal revenue and confronting balance-of-payments problems, various import protection measures arc also used in SSA countries as instruments of industrial policy. These countries are justifiably concerned with the survival and future development of an efficient manufacturing sector as an important component of their development. In this context, some level of protection may need to be given to these import-competing activities, on traditional 'infant-industry' (or, in this case, 'infant-sector') grounds, provided it is understood that the theoretical justification for such protection also requires that it be temporary and thus strictly time-bound. This reflects the idea that while the protected activities are not internationally competitive in the short term, they have potential to become competitive in the medium term. Furthermore, import protection offered on these grounds may also be differentiated to favour particular sub-sectors of the economy that exhibit positive externalities.

These two important considerations argue the case for some non-zero import tariff levels and a non-uniform import tariff structure. At the same time, however, considerations of allocative efficiency suggest that the level of import protection should be moderate to limit the relative price distortions they can create and hence the damage they can do to the economy (Rodrik, 1988). The tariff structure should be fairly simple, reflecting a limited number of tariff rates, to ensure greater transparency (Helleiner, 1992).

Given its significant implications for fiscal deficits, balance-of-payments pressures and the need for some degree of industrial protection, the future direction, scope and speed of import liberalization in SSA are likely to be influenced by the relative weights attached by policy-makers to these concerns.

Export Promotion

The export component of trade liberalization also deserves close scrutiny. This derives from the proposition that good export performance is not just a desirable goal in its own right, but is also a critical means to other important ends: that is, deeper import liberalization and more robust overall economic growth. A successful and sustainable import liberalization programme requires successful exports; or put differently, a country must export in order to import (Hachette, 1991; Snape, 1991). In the words of Michaely (1991, p. 123):

> the survival of trade liberalization attempts tends strongly to be related to a favourable export performance, whereas the collapse of trade liberalization is overwhelmingly connected with a dismal export performance.

As it relates to the export sector, trade liberalization would cover policy changes that produce a neutral trade regime that treats exportables and importables similarly as well as an 'outward-orientated' trade regime that favours and actively promotes exports. Establishing a 'neutral', not to talk of an 'outward-orientated' trade regime, as defined above, in the presence of some degree of import protection is not straightforward. Those policy measures that endow a trade regime with its import protectiveness, such as tariffs and non-tariff barriers, have an anti-export bias. More specifically, restrictions on imports translate effectively into a tax on exports; by making import substitutes relatively more profitable. They increase the costs and reduce the availability of imported inputs used in the production of exportables, forcing exporters to use relatively expensive and low quality locally produced inputs. Import restrictions also subject exporters to a more appreciated exchange rate than they would otherwise have faced. These different elements of the tax on exports imposed by import restrictions combine to reduce the international competitiveness of the export sector.

To promote exports, the anti-export bias that inherently characterizes a trade regime containing a degree of import protection needs to be eliminated. This can be done through schemes that grant exporters and their suppliers unrestricted access to inputs (imported and locally produced) at internationally-competitive prices that are free of import duty and other indirect taxes. Effective systems to provide 'neutral' trade regimes for exporters may be established in the framework of specially created export processing zones. Or, this can be done more simply through duty drawback or exemption schemes as well as bonded warehousing arrangements.

Given the widely recognized role of foreign exchange reserves and export performance in the initiation and sustainability of deep import liberalization, an important question is whether a stage of export promotion aimed at boosting exports should precede that of import liberalization (Shepherd and Langoni, 1991; Nash, 1992). This isssue derives an additional relevance from the heavy emphasis on the conventional model of trade liberalization on opening the domestic economy to competition from imports (Coes, 1991).

Based broadly on the notion that, in foreign exchange constrained economies, exports can be regarded as a means of acquiring the foreign exchange with which to purchase increased imports made available through trade liberalization, it is suggested (Nash, 1992, p. 63) that 'introducing other export policy reform shortly before, or at least at the same time as, import reforms permits an earlier export supply response and allows unification of the tariff structure to proceed without burdening exporters.

This principle appears to have featured prominently in the trade liberalization experiences of several countries. Thus, Coes (1991, p. 16) reports that:

> an important feature of the process that opened Brazil to world markets between 1964 and 1974 was the emphasis given to export – not just to the removal of restrictions on imports, as in liberalization of a purely orthodox and conventional kind. . . . Reforms in import policy came later, only after an improvement in Brazil's current account.

Similarly, Cavallo (1991, p. 31) points out that, in Argentina:

> the program of trade liberalization was a two-stage reform. During the first stage (1976–1978), commercial policies relied more heavily on export liberalization and export promotion than on competitive tariff reduction. It was only during the second stage (1979–1981) that tariffs were allowed to fall competitively, albeit in a gradual and discriminatory fashion.

There are, of course, other contrasting experiences. For instance, Hachette (1991, p. 51) finds that 'the behaviour of exports was crucial in the success of the liberalization episode in Chile; however, it was not the result of a special policy phase designed for that purpose. In his broader review of the trade liberalization experiences of several countries, Michaely (1991, p. 123) concludes that:

> no systematic connection, however, seems to exist between the adoption of export-promotion measures, as a component of the trade liberalization package, and the sustainability of a liberalization policy. Nor does the introduction of an export-promotion policy before import liberalization seem to add materially to the likelihood that trade reform will survive.

Even these contrasting experiences acknowledge the pivotal role of good export performance in sustaining import liberalization. Hence, whenever the required export performance can be more readily induced through specific export promotion measures, it would be reasonable to implement them before deeper import liberalization is implemented. In countries with clearly defined development strategies and adequate capacity to implement them, appropriate export promotion measures can be used to achieve trade 'neutrality' and thus secure outward-orientation prior to full-scale import liberalization (Levy, 1993).

Trade Liberalization: Speed and Sequencing

In any case, full-scale import liberalization is not normally achieved in one step, even in those countries (such as Chile) that choose to adopt a rapid trade liberalization process. Both theory and experience suggest a sequence that reflects the key elements of the process. These include a change in the form of protection, the simplification of the system of protection, lowering of tariff rates and reduction in the dispersion of protection rates. In this context, Helleiner (1995, p. 74) refers to 'the conventionally recommended sequence, beginning with the gradual reduction and removal of import quotas and licences and their replacement with tariffs. . ., followed by the lowering and simplification of tariffs. . . .'

Replacing quantitative restriction with tariffs, or tariffication, is in itself a major element of trade liberalization. It enhances the transparency of the system of protection. Compared to non-tariff barriers, tariffs are more visible and predictable and, hence, less susceptible to corruptive manipulation. In addition, tariffs generate government revenue and should, to that extent, help to remove some of the fiscal objections to trade liberalization. Given the clear superiority of tariffs over non-tariff barriers, countries that choose to use trade protection should rely on tariffs.

The next step in the import-liberalization process can be rapid or gradual. In general, it seems reasonable to suggest that the speed with which the rationalization and lowering of tariffs should be achieved would depend on each country's initial conditions and the response of its export sector. A gradualist approach may, obviously, run the risk of 'capture' and frustration by vested interest; this possibility provides the main argument for 'shock therapy'. Analysts who propose rapid trade liberalization tend also to indicate quite specific target and time tables. Thus, Valdes (1993, p. 280) suggests that a country undergoing trade liberalization should not only announce its programme of tariff reductions in advance, but also accomplish its tariff reduction target 'in not more than approximately three years'. This rigid schedule requires that the likely import surges associated with deep and rapid trade liberalization can be financed either by a comfortable level of foreign exchange earnings and reserves or through an adequate level of foreign assistance. Countries that cannot count on such assured, adequate and sustainable level of import financing should necessarily be more circumspect with regard to both the speed of tariff reduction and the ultimate target level envisaged in their trade liberalization programmes.

Trade Liberalization Modalities

Trade liberalization can be carried out unilaterally; it may also be implemented in the context of bilateral, regional or multilateral (global) arrangements. There is a sense in which these different trade liberalization mechanisms and modalities are related and they can be usefully integrated, wholly or partly, in a country's trade policy strategy. As argued in Tussie and Glover (1993, p. 227):

> When tariffs are very high, there are real economic gains to unilateral liberalization. This is desirable trade policy for one's own good and therefore not a real bargaining chip. Yet once trade barriers are cut back to reasonable levels, the additional efficiency gains become marginal. It is this stage, when further reductions will mean a diminished impact on efficiency, that the design of a bargaining strategy is essential.

The strategic elements that characterize trade liberalization in the context of regional and multilateral agreements include peer pressure and reciprocal actions that help participating countries to lock in the achievements of liberalization. Reciprocity enables each country to take liberalized policy actions that they would otherwise hesitate to take unilaterally. Such policy measures become less susceptible to pressures from local anti-reform interest groups in each country, while the fear of group penalty renders each country's policy largely irreversible. More specifically, multilateral trade liberalization commitments entered into through GATT/WTO negotiations provide an opportunity for countries to go beyond their unilateral liberalization efforts in exchange for multilateral concessions. They can also be used to support domestic trade reform efforts as they offer an international framework for binding these reforms and thus preventing policy reversals.

An important new dimension of the strategic element to African trade policy has recently emerged (Collier and Gunning, 1995; Fine and Yeo, 1997). Based on the observations that trade liberalization in the context of regional arrangements has had little or no success, while unilateral trade liberalization measures implemented with donor support in the context of structural adjustment programmes often lack credibility and are suseptible to reversal, it is suggested that African trade liberalization efforts may be more credible, sustainable and, hence, successful if designed and implemented in the context of a free trade area that links Africa with Europe. This reciprocal arrangement would provide as much gain as the region can expect from multilateral or global free trade, given Africa's current and prospective export markets. It would also serve the defensive purpose of protecting the region from being locked out of an emerging world of trade blocs, and provide a powerful lock-in mechanism that ensures credibility.

6.3 AFRICAN TRADE LIBERALIZATION EXPERIENCE

Trade liberalization in many of the countries of the subSaharan African region has occurred in the context of a fairly broad and general phenomenon. Since the mid-1980s, a marked shift from inward-looking regimes and controls towards outward-orientated and more open trade regimes has characterized the trade policies of most developing countries world-wide. This common trend does not, of course, imply that the trade liberalization experience has been the same in different countries and across various regions. In fact, there are significant differences along such dimensions as the motivations for trade liberalization, the initial conditions from which different countries started their liberalization process as well as the scope, speed and sequencing that various countries have chosen for reforming their trade regimes. The trade liberalization experience of SSA countries is reviewed, in this section, bearing in mind these various dimensions.

During the 1960s and 1970s, many SSA countries rapidly built up, in a rather haphazard manner, highly interventionist and protectionist trade regimes. These regimes were broadly characterized, on the import side, by restrictive licensing systems, fairly high tariffs, escalated or cascading tariff structures made up of several layers, varying degrees of import prohibitions, and tight foreign exchange controls. On the export side, the trade regimes featured substantial implicit and explicit taxes as well as frequent use of non-tariff barriers such as export prohibition.

These heavily protectionist trade regimes were motivated apparently, by several different concerns. The multiplicity of objectives, quite a few of which were conflicting, probably accounts for the rather haphazard, incoherent and internally inconsistent nature of the trade regimes that eventually emerged in many SSA countries. One of the key concerns that trade policy had to address in many SSA countries was the raising of government revenue. Given the heavy reliance of these countries on tariffs for revenue, it is not surprising that fiscal concern served as the primary motive for imposing high tariff rates on both imports and exports. At the same time, these countries were highly susceptible to balance-of-payments pressure, given their strong commitments to the maintenance of often unrealistic fixed exchange rate systems. In this context, trade policy often became a substitute for more appropriate policies needed to maintain macroeconomic discipline (such as exchange rate policy reform, for instance). Hence, non-tariff import controls were often applied whenever it became necessary to deal with recurring balance-of-payment crises. This is clearly consistent with the evidence that some 80 per cent of the quantitative import restrictions notified to the GATT by SSA countries during the 1970s and early 1980s were justified for balance-of-payments reasons under GATT Article XVIII.B.

Some aspects of SSA's protectionist trade regimes in the 1960s and 1970s could also be traced to the desire to shelter domestic industry, as a means of enhancing overall development, in the context of the import-substitution industrialization (ISI) strategy which was quite popular at the time. Evidence in support of this include extensive exemption from duties and low tariff rates for imported inputs used by local producers, as well as the generally escalated structure of tariffs that imposed high rates on finished products and much lower rates on raw materials. It should be noted, however, that tariff rates were applied to so-called 'luxury' goods thought to be consumed largely by the rich and for which no local production facility existed. Thus, high tariff rates did not always reflect the desire to protect local industry; in certain cases they reflected the desire to raise revenue based on perceived ability of the consumer to pay.

There is a strong relationship between the use of import restrictions and the appearance of balance-of-payments problems in many SSA countries; while the increasing significance of border taxes as a contributor to government revenue can be matched with the rising level of import tariff rates in these countries up to the early 1980s. Taken together, these relationships and trends suggest that budgetary needs and balance-of-payments concerns had much stronger impact on the evolution and structure of the trade regime in SSA countries than the desire to protect local industry.

Beginning around the mid-1980s, many SSA countries started the difficult journey of rationalizing and liberalizing their trade regimes. They have been guided and prodded along on this journey by the World Bank and the IMF in the context of integrated packages of economic policy and associated reforms conventionally referred to as structural adjustment programmes. In spite of this common source of stimuli, progress across the countries involved has been uneven, while the sequencing of the liberalization process has been problematic. Many of the liberalization attempts have not followed the standard sequence of replacing quantitative restrictions with high (equivalent) tariff rates first before adjusting the tariffs towards lower and more uniform levels subsequently and in a phased manner.

The liberalization efforts have generally concentrated on the import side and have, to that extent, paid much less attention to the elimination of anti-export bias inherent in the trade regime. There is clear evidence, however, that 'protection of import substitutes by tariffs and non-tariff barriers (NTBs) in Sub-Saharan Africa as a whole has declined' (Nash, 1993, p. 38). More specifically, the level of protection has fallen by between 30 per cent and 50 per cent over the period from the mid-1980s to the early 1990s, and the downward trend has continued through the mid-1990s. Thus, a more recent assessment (World Bank, 1995, p. 24) finds that 'since the mid-1980s, most African countries have moved from complete or nearly complete government control over imports to more open systems, and have substantially reduce the number of imports subject to quantitative bearers'. It goes on to indicate that:

> the greatest progress has been achieved in replacing quantitative restrictions with lower and less dispersed tariff levels; more than half the countries now have average tariff rates of 15–20 present with the highest rates set at 35–40 per cent, and the number of tariff categories reduced to 4–5.

But on the export side, the picture is much less favourable, According to Nash (1993, p. 42): 'there has been little progress on establishing efficient systems to give exporters access to inputs at internationally competitive prices' since the various institutional mechanisms for achieving this objective, such as export-processing zones or duty drawback and exemption schemes, remain underdeveloped in virtually all SSA countries.

6.4 THE WAY FORWARD

The trade regimes of many SSA countries in the 1960s and 1970s evolved through an *ad hoc* and haphazard process; they reflect attempts to use one instrument (that is, trade policy) to achieve several (and, sometimes, inconsistent) objectives. The policy reforms which began in the mid-1980s and are, in many cases, still on-going have achieved some significant results but much still remains to be done, especially in terms of *rationalizing* the trade regimes. In order that further policy reforms may be effective, they should be designed and implemented in the context of a comprehensive framework that takes account of the initial conditions in each country, its long-term development objectives and the strategy for achieving them. It is within this context that one should pose the questions: What role can trade policy play? What direction, scope, and sequencing of trade policy reform is indicated?

A broad consensus has emerged which indicates that, in the long term, development in SSA countries should focus on the achievement of rapid, equitable and sustainable economic growth (World Bank, 1995). Both theories and accumulated experience of successful development experience elsewhere (for example, East Asia) suggest that a realistic overall development strategy for achieving this growth objective should stress broad outward-orientation. The peculiar characteristics of most SSA countries as small and historically 'open' economies (in the sense of high ratios of trade to GDP) are broadly consistent with this focus. SSA's failed experiment with its largely inward-orientated development strategy of the 1960s and 1970s should also quite rightly provide an additional support for a radical change in orientation. An outward-orientated development strategy assumes that aggregate economic growth will be export-led in an environment in which macroeconomic balance and stability are maintained.

Development experience world-wide suggests that industrialization plays a significant role in the process of establishing rapid and sustained economic growth; the current marginalization of SSA in this respect would have to be addressed if the regions long-term development objective is to be achieved. The initial conditions regarding industrialization in many SSA countries become particularly relevant at this juncture. The region's previous import-substitution industrialization strategy has not only failed to deliver sustainable growth of the manufacturing sector but it has also created a difficult legacy of massive inefficiency and heavy import-dependence that needs to be overcome before a new push in promoting industrialization could worth while. More specifically, promoting export-orientated industrialization against the background of the ISI legacy requires (1) restructuring the existing manufacturing sector whose structure and efficiency levels are ill-suited to exporting; (2) altering the incentive regime to provide exporters with access to inputs at international prices net of tariffs and indirect taxes; and (3) using appropriate pro-active measures to assist manufacturers and exporters to cope with the production and learning-by-doing externalities associated with manufacturing and the difficulties of gaining access to the information and technology needed to break into export markets (Lall and Stewart, 1995).

The initial conditions of SSA and its long-term development objective and strategy briefly sketched above provide the context within which future trade policy reform can be meaningfully discussed. This should begin with the recognition that credible and balanced macroeconomic policies are essential for reaping the benefits of trade liberalization. In any case, the prior achievement and continuous maintenance of macroeconomic balance and stability would release standard trade policy instruments from inappropriately chasing revenue and balance-of-payments objectives and enable them to concentrate on the more legitimate role of enhancing efficiency in resource allocation and promoting long-term development via industrialization and export expansion and diversification.

Trade policy instruments would not be released from the duty of chasing revenue objectives until the importance of border taxes in the tax system is significantly reduced. This can be achieved through increased reliance on a substantially revamped domestic indirect tax system which, for example, replaces the existing patchwork of sales taxes with a more comprehensive value-added-tax. Similarly, a more flexible and responsive exchange rate policy backed with adequate financing is necessary if trade liberalization is to be consistent with the maintenance of balance-of-payments stability. Deep import liberalization cannot be sustained and would not be viewed by private agents as credible in the absence of these conditions.

Following the establishment of macroeconomic balance and stability, full import liberalization would be the first best way to eliminate anti-export bias and thus promote exports. But, given the existence of some manufacturing capacity in many SSA countries part of which could be restructured, revived and transformed into export-orientated local production facilities, a certain degree of protection should be retained. The inherent anti-export bias in the resulting trade regime should be compensated for by providing direct and indirect exporters access to imported inputs at international prices through the effective use of such institutional mechanims as export processing zones, in-bond warehousing, and duty drawback and exemption schemes.

Future trade liberalization programmes in SSA would be more credible and effective if they emanate from clearly articulated and coherent strategies that explicitly recognize specific objectives and address both the import and export sides of the trade 'coin'. Similarly, the context in which trade liberalization programmes are implemented could have significant implications for their success and sustainability. Most of SSA's recent trade liberalization efforts have been based on structural adjustment programmes, supported by the World Bank. The basic model that underpins these programmes assumes that adjusting countries would 'receive balance of payments assistance equivalent to 20–50 per cent of exports earnings' (Harrold *et al.*, 1995, p. 89). As Collier and Gunning (1995) convincingly argue, such aid-induced trade liberalization attempts may not be credible and therefore suffer reversal because the 'inducement' is not permanent and its temporary nature is quickly recognised by private agents. In comparison, credibility of trade liberalization is enhanced when it is implemented in the context of a 'reciprocal-threat' arrangement in which the certain reactions of partners make unilateral policy reversal costly. Hence, the credibility of future trade liberalization attempts in SSA is likely to be enhanced to the extend that they are 'GATT-bound' or are implemented within the terms of effective regional integration (including north–south reciprocal) schemes.

References

Cavallo, D. F. (1991) 'Argentina: Trade Reform, 1976–1982', in G. Shepherd and C. G. Langoni (eds), *Trade Reform: Lessons from Eight Countries* (San Francisco: ICEG).

Coes, D. (1991) 'Brazil: Precedents and Prospects in Foreign Trade', in G. Shepherd and C. G. Langoni (eds), *Trade Reform: Lessons from Eight Countries* (San Francisco: ICEG).

Collier, P. and J. W. Gunning (1992) 'Aid and Exchange Rate Adjustment in African Trade Liberalization', *Economic Journal*, **102**: 925–39.

Collier, P. and J. W. Gunning (1995) 'Trade Policy and Regional Integration: Implications for the Relations between Europe and Africa', *The World Economy*, 18: 387–410.

Fine, J. and S. Yeo (1997) 'Regional Integration in SubSaharan Africa: Dead End or a Fresh Start?' in A. Oyejide, I. Elbadawi and P. Collier (eds) *Regional Integration and Trade Liberalization in SubSaharan Africa. Vol. 1: Framework, Issues and Methodological Perspectives* (London: Macmillan).

Hachette, D. (1991) 'Chile: Trade Liberalization since 1974', in G. Shepherd and C. G. Langoni (eds), *Trade Reform: Lessons from Eight Countries* (San Francisco: ICEG).

Harrold, P., M. Jayawickrama, and D. Bhattasali (1995) *Practical Lessons for Africa From East Asia in Industrial and Trade Policies*, World Bank Discussion Papers, Africa Technical Department Series (Washington, DC: World Bank).

Helleiner, G. K. (1992) 'Introduction', in G. K. Helleiner (ed.), *Trade Policy, Industrialization and Development: New Perspectives* (Oxford: Clarendon Press).

Helleiner, G. K. (1995) *Trade, Trade Policy and Industrialization Reconsidered*, World Development Studies no. 6 (Helsinki: wider [UNU]).

Lall, S. and F. Stewart (1995) 'Trade and Industrial Policy in Africa' Johannesburg: North South Roundtable).

Levy, B. (1993) 'An Institutional Analysis of the Design and Sequence of Trade and Investment Policy Reform', *World Bank Economic Review*, **7**(2): 247–62.

Lyakurwa, W. M. (1993) *Trade Policy and Promotion in Sub-Saharan Africa*, Special Paper no. 12 (Nairobi: AERC).

Michaely, M. (1991) 'The Lessons of Experience: An Overview', in G. Shepherd and C. G. Langoni (eds), *Trade Reform: Lessons From Eight Countries* (San Francisco: ICEG).

Nash, J. (1992) 'An Overview of Trade Policy Reform, with Implications for Sub-Saharan Africa', in J.-M. Fontaine (ed.), *Foreign Trade Reforms and Development Strategy* (London and New York: Routledge).

Nash, J. (1993) 'Trade Policy Reform Implementation in Sub-Saharan Africa: How Much Heat and How Much Light?, mimeo (Washington, DC: World Bank).

Rodrik, D. (1988) 'Imperfect Competition, Scale Economies, and Trade Policy in Developing Countries', in R. E. Baldwin (ed.), *Trade Policy Issues and Empirical Analysis* (University of Chicago Press).

Shepherd, G. and C. G. Langoni (eds) (1991) *Trade Reform: Lessons From Eight Countries* (San Francisco: ICEG).

Snape, R. H. (1991) 'Fast Asia: Trade Reform in Korea and Singapore', in G. Shepherd and C. G. Langoni (eds), *Trade Reform: Lessons From Eight Countries* (San Francisco: ICEG).

Tussie, D. and D. Glover (eds) (1993) *The Developing Countries in World Trade: Policies and Bargaining Strategies* (Ottawa: IDRC).

Valdes, A. (1993) 'The Macroeconomic Environment Necessary For Agricultural Trade and Price Policy Reforms', *Food Policy* (August): 272–83.

World Bank, The (1981) *Accelerated Development in Sub-Saharan Africa: An Agenda For Action* (Washington, DC: World Bank).

World Bank, The (1991) *World Development Report: The Challenge of Development* (New York: Oxford University Press).

World Bank, The (1992) *Trade Policy Reforms Under Structural Adjustment* (Washington, DC: World Bank).

World Bank, The (1995) *A Continent in Transition: Sub-Saharan African in the mid-1990s* (Washington, DC: World Bank).

Contents of Volumes 1, 2 and 3

Volume 1 Framework, Issues and Methodological Perspectives

Volume 2 Country Case-Studies

Volume 3 Regional Case-Studies

Index

Note: page numbers in **bold** type refer to tabular matter.